Llewellyn's Witches' Datebook 2019

Featuring

Art by Kathleen Edwards
Text by Elizabeth Barrette, Blake Octavian Blair,
Monica Crosson, Autumn Damiana, Raven Digitalis,
Estha K. V. McNevin, Mickie Mueller, Diana Rajchel,
Charlynn Walls, and Natalie Zaman

ISBN 978-0-7387-4616-6

2019

JANUARY	FEBRUARY	MARCH	APRIL
S M T W T F S	S M T W T F S	S M T W T F S	S M T W T F S
1 2 3 4 5	1 2	1 2	1 2 3 4 5 6
6 7 8 9 10 11 12	3 4 5 6 7 8 9	3 4 5 6 7 8 9	7 8 9 10 11 12 13
13 14 15 16 17 18 19	10 11 12 13 14 15 16	10 11 12 13 14 15 16	14 15 16 17 18 19 20
20 21 22 23 24 25 26	17 18 19 20 21 22 23	17 18 19 20 21 22 23	21 22 23 24 25 26 27
27 28 29 30 31	24 25 26 27 28	24 25 26 27 28 29 30 / 31	28 29 30

MAY	JUNE	JULY	AUGUST
S M T W T F S	S M T W T F S	S M T W T F S	S M T W T F S
1 2 3 4	1	1 2 3 4 5 6	1 2 3
5 6 7 8 9 10 11	2 3 4 5 6 7 8	7 8 9 10 11 12 13	4 5 6 7 8 9 10
12 13 14 15 16 17 18	9 10 11 12 13 14 15	14 15 16 17 18 19 20	11 12 13 14 15 16 17
19 20 21 22 23 24 25	16 17 18 19 20 21 22	21 22 23 24 25 26 27	18 19 20 21 22 23 24
26 27 28 29 30 31	23 24 25 26 27 28 29 / 30	28 29 30 31	25 26 27 28 29 30 31

SEPTEMBER	OCTOBER	NOVEMBER	DECEMBER
S M T W T F S	S M T W T F S	S M T W T F S	S M T W T F S
1 2 3 4 5 6 7	1 2 3 4 5	1 2	1 2 3 4 5 6 7
8 9 10 11 12 13 14	6 7 8 9 10 11 12	3 4 5 6 7 8 9	8 9 10 11 12 13 14
15 16 17 18 19 20 21	13 14 15 16 17 18 19	10 11 12 13 14 15 16	15 16 17 18 19 20 21
22 23 24 25 26 27 28	20 21 22 23 24 25 26	17 18 19 20 21 22 23	22 23 24 25 26 27 28
29 30	27 28 29 30 31	24 25 26 27 28 29 30	29 30 31

2020

JANUARY	FEBRUARY	MARCH	APRIL
S M T W T F S	S M T W T F S	S M T W T F S	S M T W T F S
1 2 3 4	1	1 2 3 4 5 6 7	1 2 3 4
5 6 7 8 9 10 11	2 3 4 5 6 7 8	8 9 10 11 12 13 14	5 6 7 8 9 10 11
12 13 14 15 16 17 18	9 10 11 12 13 14 15	15 16 17 18 19 20 21	12 13 14 15 16 17 18
19 20 21 22 23 24 25	16 17 18 19 20 21 22	22 23 24 25 26 27 28	19 20 21 22 23 24 25
26 27 28 29 30 31	23 24 25 26 27 28 29	29 30 31	26 27 28 29 30

MAY	JUNE	JULY	AUGUST
S M T W T F S	S M T W T F S	S M T W T F S	S M T W T F S
1 2	1 2 3 4 5 6	1 2 3 4	1
3 4 5 6 7 8 9	7 8 9 10 11 12 13	5 6 7 8 9 10 11	2 3 4 5 6 7 8
10 11 12 13 14 15 16	14 15 16 17 18 19 20	12 13 14 15 16 17 18	9 10 11 12 13 14 15
17 18 19 20 21 22 23	21 22 23 24 25 26 27	19 20 21 22 23 24 25	16 17 18 19 20 21 22
24 25 26 27 28 29 30 / 31	28 29 30	26 27 28 29 30 31	23 24 25 26 27 28 29 / 30 31

SEPTEMBER	OCTOBER	NOVEMBER	DECEMBER
S M T W T F S	S M T W T F S	S M T W T F S	S M T W T F S
1 2 3 4 5	1 2 3	1 2 3 4 5 6 7	1 2 3 4 5
6 7 8 9 10 11 12	4 5 6 7 8 9 10	8 9 10 11 12 13 14	6 7 8 9 10 11 12
13 14 15 16 17 18 19	11 12 13 14 15 16 17	15 16 17 18 19 20 21	13 14 15 16 17 18 19
20 21 22 23 24 25 26	18 19 20 21 22 23 24	22 23 24 25 26 27 28	20 21 22 23 24 25 26
27 28 29 30	25 26 27 28 29 30 31	29 30	27 28 29 30 31

Llewellyn's Witches' Datebook 2019 © 2018 by Llewellyn Publications, 2143 Wooddale Dr., Dept. 978-0-7387-4616-6, Woodbury, MN 55125-2989. All rights reserved. No part of this publication may be reproduced in any form without the permission of the publisher, except for quotations used in critical reviews. Llewellyn Publications is a registered trademark of Llewellyn Worldwide Ltd.

Editing and layout by Lauryn Heineman

Cover illustration and interior art © 2018 by Kathleen Edwards

Art on chapter openings © 2006 by Jennifer Hewitson

Art direction by Lynne Menturweck

Table of Contents

How to Use *Llewellyn's Witches' Datebook* 4
For the Birds *by Monica Crosson* 6
Visualization Using All Five Senses *by Autumn Damiana* 11
After the Offering *by Blake Octavian Blair* 15
Eisenhower Grids for Witches *by Diana Rajchel* 19
Positions of Power *by Charlynn Walls* 24
January 28
February 38
March 48
April 60
May 70
June 80
July 92
August 102
September 114
October 124
November 134
December 146
About the Contributors 158
Appendix 160
Notes 166

How to Use Llewellyn's Witches' Datebook

Welcome to *Llewellyn's Witches' Datebook 2019!* This datebook was designed especially for Witches, Pagans, and magical people. Use it to plan sabbat celebrations, magic, Full Moon rites, and even dentist and doctor appointments. At right is a symbol key to some of the features of this datebook.

MOON QUARTERS: The Moon's cycle is divided into four quarters, which are noted in the weekly pages along with their exact times. When the Moon changes quarter, both quarters are listed, as well as the time of the change. In addition, a symbol for the new quarter is placed where the numeral for the date usually appears.

MOON IN THE SIGNS: Approximately every two and a half days, the Moon moves from one zodiac sign to the next. The sign that the Moon is in at the beginning of the day (midnight Eastern Time) is noted next to the quarter listing. If the Moon changes signs that day, there will be a notation saying "☽ enters" followed by the symbol for the sign it is entering.

MOON VOID-OF-COURSE: Just before the Moon enters a new sign, it will make one final aspect (angular relationship) to another planet. Between that last aspect and the entrance of the Moon into the next sign it is said to be void-of-course. Activities begun when the Moon is void-of-course rarely come to fruition, or they turn out very differently than planned.

PLANETARY MOVEMENT: When a planet or asteroid moves from one sign into another, this change (called an *ingress*) is noted on the calendar pages with the exact time. The Moon and Sun are considered planets in this case. The planets (except for the Sun and Moon) can also appear to move backward as seen from the Earth. This is called a *planetary retrograde*, and is noted on the calendar pages with the symbol ℞. When the planet begins to move forward, or direct, again, it is marked D, and the time is also noted.

PLANTING AND HARVESTING DAYS: The best days for planting and harvesting are noted on the calendar pages with a seedling icon (planting) and a basket icon (harvesting).

TIME ZONE CHANGES: The times and dates of all astrological phenomena in this datebook are based on Eastern time. If you live outside the Eastern time zone, you will need to make the following changes: Pacific Time subtract three hours; Mountain Time subtract two hours; Central Time subtract one hour; Alaska subtract four hours; and Hawaii subtract five hours. All data is adjusted for Daylight Saving Time.

Planets

- ☉ Sun
- ☽ Moon
- ☿ Mercury
- ♀ Venus
- ♂ Mars
- ♃ Jupiter
- ♄ Saturn
- ♅ Uranus
- ♆ Neptune
- ♇ Pluto
- ⚷ Chiron
- ⚳ Ceres
- ⚴ Pallas
- ⚵ Juno
- ⚶ Vesta

Signs

- ♈ Aries
- ♉ Taurus
- ♊ Gemini
- ♋ Cancer
- ♌ Leo
- ♍ Virgo
- ♎ Libra
- ♏ Scorpio
- ♐ Sagittarius
- ♑ Capricorn
- ♒ Aquarius
- ♓ Pisces

Motion

- ℞ Retrograde
- D Direct

1st Quarter/New Moon ☽
2nd Quarter ◐
3rd Quarter/Full Moon ☺
4th Quarter ◑

For the Birds
by Monica Crosson

It was an afternoon in mid-October, when the maples were attired in their autumn finery and the Sun still garnered enough strength to convince me to peel off layers that were so desperately needed in the morning, that I pulled into our driveway after finishing up a few errands in town. My four-year-old son, Joshua, ran out to greet me, as he did every time I escaped for a little time alone. He was cheering and waving as he always did, but there was something unusual about his attire. Propped on his shoulder was something quite large and black. I thought it might be a toy, part of some game he was playing, but then it moved. I blinked. *Was that a bird?* I rubbed my eyes and looked again. Yes, there was a crow on my son's shoulder.

"Mama, Mama," my son called, "I got a new pet. He just flew to me." The crow croaked, as if in agreement.

I looked at my husband, Steve, who had just stepped off the front porch, grinning. "It's true," he said. "We were in the backyard when this crow swooped at Joshua from the forest and landed on his shoulder."

I reached down to pet the little beauty, but with a flurry of feathers and a couple of croaks, he was suddenly on my own shoulder, contentedly picking at my hair.

"There you go," Steve said. "You've always said you wished you had a raven or crow as a pet. Now you've got one."

I smiled and stroked his ebony head. Steve was right, I had always wanted one. I always thought I would name him Arthur, and my feathered familiar would escort me to ritual or join me for walks along the riverbank. I smiled, despite his strange arrival. "Arthur," I spoke softly to him. He croaked gently in response. "Welcome to the family."

The gravelly voice of my four-year-old interrupted my moment: "His name is Blackhead."

"Wait. What?" Fantasy blown. "Like a pimple?"

"No, Mom. Because he has a black head." The crow flew back to Joshua, this time landing squarely on his head . . . traitor.

"Well, don't you think Arthur is a better-suited name for him?" I tried to convince my son. "Just like in the stories of King Arthur and Merlin?"

Joshua thought for a moment. "Um, no. I think his name should be Blackhead because he's so black."

"Yeah, Mom," Steve said, obviously enjoying my pain. "Besides, what if the crow's a girl? Arthur is a boy's name. Blackhead can be a girl's name or boy's name."

"Yeah, Mom." Joshua joined in.

"Okay." I sighed, knowing it was time to give in. "Welcome to the family . . . Blackhead."

Navigator between Worlds

Birds have long been linked with the Divine, playing a central role in many creation myths and lending their attributes to gods and goddesses throughout antiquity. In some versions of her myth, the Egyptian goddess Isis used her wings to fan life into Osiris. The Norse goddess Freya owned a garment of feathers that enabled magicians to fly when they wore it, and the Celtic goddess Rhiannon was accompanied by birds whose song led the dying sweetly into death. The Egyptian god Ra was born in an egg, and the Celtic god Lugh was associated with the eagle, raven, and crow.

In shamanism birds serve as a symbol of magickal flight and are navigators between worlds. Clothing and ritual tools are often made from or ornamented with the feathers, bones, or beaks of birds, aiding the shaman in summoning the bird's power to contact other realms.

Birds were the givers of omens, carriers of souls, and holders of secrets for our ancient ancestors, so there were many forms of divination connected to birds. Oomancia was the art of divining the future through eggs, and augury used the flight patterns, songs, and entrails of birds to guide in predictions. According to myth, the location of the site for Rome was divined by the flight patterns of birds, and weather predictions using birds were used up until the last one hundred years.

Birds played an integral role in the spiritual belief systems of almost every culture in the past. But what about today? Watching and connecting with the power of birds is one way to draw us back to nature and deepen our own connection with the Divine. One way to reconnect with bird energy is by creating a backyard bird habitat. Believe me, the birds (and other wildlife) will be thankful, and you will feel a much more harmonious energy around your home and yard.

Creating a Bird Habitat

In today's world, most lawns have been primped and trimmed to cookie-cutter perfection; more than a shocking seventy million gallons of pesticides are used yearly to maintain these green carpets. Sadly, our need for the perfect yard is not only poisoning the environment, but it is also partly responsible for increasing habitat loss for our feathered friends. Creating a space with native plants, grasses, shrubs, trees, and a water feature provides much-needed food, shelter, and nesting places for local birds. It also creates a space for us to relax, observe, and connect with the birds' powerful energy. Here are a few things to consider when creating a bird habitat:

Multilayered canopy: Choose trees, shrubs, and vines of varying heights. Taller trees provide crucial resting or nesting areas, while shrubs and vines provide a nice shelter from predators. Another thing to consider is fruit-bearing shrubs and vines. They make a great food source for birds such as thrushes, robins, and waxwings.

Grasses and flowering perennials: These flowering plants that come back year after year not only provide cover for our feathered friends, but their seeds are also a much-needed food source. Don't forget to plant annual favorites such as sunflower and bachelor's button.

Water source: A birdbath, small pond, fountain, or even a large saucer provides a place for drinking and bathing.

Bird feeders and nesting boxes: To offer a varied diet and to attract specific bird species to your yard, try putting out bird feeders with nuts, seeds, and fruits specific to your local birds' needs. Do some research and hang nesting boxes that will help foster interest from local species. Let the kids get involved by decorating small birdhouses with Witchy symbols before hanging to lend a magickal feel to your environment.

Remember, even if you don't have a traditional grassy yard, many small trees, shrubs, and flowering plants can be potted and placed on patios or balconies. Hang bird feeders near windows and provide nesting boxes wherever you can.

Magick Takes Flight

Now that you have created a haven to nurture your local birds, it's time to set up a sacred space to help nurture your own soul and let the birds' powerful energy help you make that connection with the Divine. Set up a small altar dedicated to the birds. Set up nests, feathers, painted eggs, bird figurines, and ornamentation of the Mother Goddess. Hang wind chimes or add a soothing water feature. Further designate this enchanted area as sacred with the following simple dedication.

I have chosen to use robin energy for this dedication ritual because of its connection with new beginnings. This one is fun for the kids because there is egg breaking involved. You will need the following:

A raw egg that you have colored blue like a robin's egg
Twigs, grass, or straw loosely formed as a nest (in a dish)
A found robin's feather (or feather of your choosing)
Hyacinth incense (representing new beginnings)

On a table near your bird habitat, set up your dish with the nest, incense (in an incense burner or a firesafe container), and feather. Light the incense. If you are doing this dedication ritual with children, let them crack the egg into the nest. As this is done, say,

Robin, please lend your energy to provide this garden with safety, serenity, and cheer to all those who fly from far and near.

Take the feather and fan the incense toward the garden. As you do this, repeat three times,

May this habitat provide shelter, may this habitat provide safety, may this habitat express love.

Bury the egg and nesting material somewhere in your habitat.

Feather Fetish

Fetishes are natural objects that can be used in your magickal practices and whose energy you feel closely associated with. As a Witch who closely associates herself with the natural world, I've found that a walk in the woods can offer a treasure trove of magickal objects—and feathers are one of my favorite fetish finds.

Feathers are ruled by the element of air. They work well in spells for communication and are often used to aid in focus and promote change. Knowing which bird your feather came from can really help refine your spellcrafting by giving form and focus on a particular energy. However, note that according to the Migratory Bird Treaty Act, it is illegal to take or possess the feathers of migratory birds. Decorating plain white feathers obtained from a craft store and using them to symbolically represent a given species is always an alternative.

Here is a list of common backyard birds you may find feathers from and their magickal correspondences:

Bluebird: happiness, confidence, transformation
Cardinal: passion, vitality, self-love
Crow: wisdom, past-life, mourning, letting go
Finch: new experiences, increased potential
Grosbeak: family values, healing old wounds
Hummingbird: finding joy, faerie magick, continuity
Owl: wisdom, self-truth, clairvoyance, occult wisdom
Robin: new growth and beginnings, fertility, domestic bliss
Sparrow: ambition, triumph, self-worth
Woodpecker: earth's rhythms, prophecy, life's cycles

Birds have always played a significant role in my life. After Blackhead slipped away quietly just over a year after his arrival, an eagle we called Einstein came into our lives for a short time. Most recently, we found two baby robins whose nest had fallen and successfully raised them and released them back into the wild. I believe fully that the universe sent them to me for a reason, and from birds I have learned that patience and wisdom go hand in hand, how to appreciate my failings—they helped me transform to who I am today—and that there is courage in letting go.

So, remember to always look to the sky—you never know what magick might be on the wing.

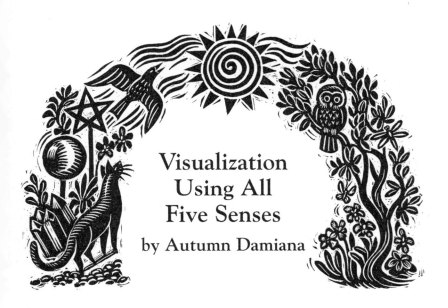

Visualization Using All Five Senses
by Autumn Damiana

Any magic practitioner will tell you that the successful casting of a spell requires focus and concentration, usually accomplished through "visualization" of your goal. This word gets used a lot in spell instructions, and some would say that if you can't effectively visualize what you want, then your spell won't work at all. But what exactly is visualization? As I see it, visualization is, essentially, imagination. Hardly anyone in the magical world wants to describe the process like this because it implies "imaginary" (or even "pretend"). And yet, this is exactly what visualization is: you see in your mind's eye something that has not yet happened—and so you imagine it into existence. Magical tools, supplies, and sacred space are often used in conjunction with imagination to make a goal manifest, and this is how spells work.

However, there's this idea that to get into a mindset for spellcasting, there is a magical "prescription" to be applied that almost always involves the same core elements: candlelight, burning incense, wearing special clothing, and so on. None of these are mandatory, but they are all recommended because they are supposed to help the subconscious get in the mood for magic and therefore aid in visualization. This may work well for some, but it's not the one-size-fits-all method of spellcasting that it is assumed to be. Not everyone will resonate with such visual aids, because not everyone can visualize in the traditional sense.

Consider how people learn: some learn by seeing (visual), some by listening (auditory), and some by doing (kinesthetic)—it's usually some combination of the three. How someone learns will naturally affect how they perceive the world around them. If you are not much of a visual learner, then how well are you going to be able to visualize a spell? The answer is simple: you should investigate a different method. This can be accomplished through using the other senses. In his theory of multiple intelligences, psychologist Howard Gardner describes nine different intelligence types that identify both a person's learning style and their intelligence strengths. These are naturalist, musical, logical-mathematical, existential, interpersonal, bodily-kinesthetic, linguistic, intrapersonal, and spatial. I recommend researching the different types to see which ones you are proficient in at http://funders andfounders.com/9-types-of-intelligence and http://www.literacynet .org/mi/assessment/findyourstrengths.html.

Now, how does this information help you become better at spellcrafting? By allowing you to discover the different stimuli needed to coax out your magical talents. Everyone is magically gifted on some level, but because visualization skills are stressed, some believe that if they cannot "see" the spell working in their mind, they are not "doing it right." This is where using all five senses comes into play. The point of visualization is to direct energy in your spell toward your goal, so how much more powerful would the spell be if you involved more of your senses? By immersing yourself completely into your visualization in this manner, you are effectively tricking your body into believing that what you imagine is true, and you will therefore be more likely to succeed in casting your spell. This idea also works well with meditations and journeying.

For instance, say that you decide to craft a spell for a vacation to an island in the Caribbean. To work the spell, you will need to imagine being there, but it will feel more believable if you also engage your other senses. So while you are picturing yourself at a seaside resort, maybe you can push your fingers into a container of sand and sip a cold fruity cocktail. Try adding coconut-scented lotion to your skin and playing a recording of gentle ocean waves. This experience should help you engage fully in your visualization much more than through mental pictures alone. And if these ideas don't appeal to you, you can easily change them. Perhaps you'd like to lounge in the sun or listen to some calypso music. Do whatever you can to create layers of sensation while you visualize.

Spellcraft Ideas for Each Sense

Sight: There are myriad accounts of individuals who experience a heightened level of sensitivity in their other abilities after losing their sight. What's more, even when doing traditional visualization, most people close their eyes in order to concentrate better! To strengthen your sense of sight, create vision boards, make collages, or try sketching your spell. Or, find an image that represents your goal and stare steadily at it, using sight to notice every line, color, and nuance so that it develops a deeper meaning for you.

Hearing: Commonly associated with language and music in spells, your sense of hearing can be used in other ways. Chants, poetry, singing, playing instruments, and listening to music or sound effects are wonderful additions, but think of all the other sounds that you hear regularly: traffic, dogs barking, construction, wind or rain, children playing, and so on. Pick out the ones you are drawn to, and record them for later use. Wind and rain may aid you in a banishing or cleansing, and the noise of children will work wonders in a fertility spell. You can also create your own sound effects—footsteps, a clock ticking, and even the sound of your own breath. The possibilities are endless.

Touch: This sense can be used a number of ways. You can physically feel tactile materials, or you can think on a more bodily or kinesthetic level. Worry stones, prayer beads, and the recent "fidgety" gadgets are so popular because touch is a sense that we take for granted, even though we rely on it constantly. Jiggle coins in your hand for a wealth spell. For healing, use an appropriate herb or flower in some warm water, place your feet in it, and draw the power up through your legs and into your body. Meticulously handling an object will also help you connect to it or program it with energy.

Taste: Don't limit yourself to just food and drink—take advantage of their distinct components. There are a lot of spells that call for individual herbs and spices that have culinary uses, so why not taste them in addition to using them in your charm bags, poppets, and potions?

Specific types of taste can also be used in your spell, even if they are not spell ingredients themselves—for example, salt for grounding, sugar to add sweetness, hot sauce for sexual energy, and so on.

Smell: In my opinion, this sense is an undervalued asset. As smell is most closely linked with memory, scent can easily be used to evoke a particular feeling or emotion. Unfortunately, the only way most ever use it while casting spells is through burning incense. Try scented oils, lotions, water spritzes, foods, herb and spice combinations, perfumes, or an embedded smell, like the cozy scent of old books.

Further Sensory Visualization Ideas

Journal about your likes and dislikes with each sense. Really give this some thought, and avoid the obvious—no one likes the smell of skunk or rotting garbage! Think of comparisons that are your opinions or gut reactions, and try recording them in pairs so that your list isn't one-sided. Maybe you like the feel of cotton, but not wool, or you like the sound of rain, but not thunder. By doing this exercise, patterns will emerge that will help you create or adapt spells more tailored to you.

Develop each sense more completely. Take a "sense vacation" by blocking out or not using one or more of the senses for a short period at a time. With a blindfold, attempt to identify each spice in your cabinet through smell alone, or sit with a box of objects and feel each one, noting the shape, weight, and texture. Use earplugs and see what changes for you without hearing. I bet you'll be surprised what you can learn by isolating the senses in this manner.

Practice mindfulness. Each of us experiences life through sensory input . . . so the next time you find yourself caught up in a moment, stop and observe what is happening. Whether it's a sight, sound, feeling, taste, or smell, being conscious of it then and there will help your visualizations later if you can clearly remember the experience. Good luck!

After the Offering
by Blake Octavian Blair

There are a number of considerations when choosing an offering in your magickal and ceremonial work. Just a few of these concerns might include magickal correspondences, what we have available to us locally, and the purpose of the offering or what divine entity it is for. However, one very important concern—one that should be at the top of the list for any earth-revering spiritual practitioner—is what to do with the offering after it has been made. While there are ceremonial and ritual protocols to be considered, the ecological impact of the offering also needs to be factored. Sadly, this important element is often overlooked.

Food and drink are some of the most common offering items across spiritual traditions. There are two obvious avenues for this type of offering post-ceremony. The first option is consumption of the offering goods by the practitioner. This is an established tradition of many spiritual paths, including modern Paganism, as in the "cakes and ale" ceremony. The practice appears in Eastern traditions such as Buddhism and Hinduism in which the food items offered to deities are eaten, and this is seen as taking in and having the deities' blessings conferred upon you by consuming the blessed food, which is referred to as *prasad*. As you might surmise, consuming the food has a fairly low environmental impact associated with disposing of the offering.

The second option, of course, is to simply dispose of the food and drink. This leads us to the discussion of the environmental impact and ecological considerations of our offerings. If we do not consume it, we often do not want to throw it in the trash after its important role in ceremony. In many contexts, that can be seen as disrespectful. However, we must consider the materials of our offerings. We can in fact find ways to dispose of the offering considerately and responsibly after the offering has been chosen and made. However, I encourage you to think about this concern before the offering is even chosen. The best offerings are, in my opinion, made of organic, biodegradable materials. A biodegradable offering can be left or buried in nature to return to the earth, and on occasion it will be picked over by wildlife. Of course, it is also important to consider the potential dangers of the material to wildlife as well.

Nature-Friendly Offerings

Many of us prefer to dispose of, deposit, or otherwise actually perform the act of offering in nature for reasons of protocol of tradition, connection to nature, or appropriateness of the working. Thus, it is ideal to choose nature-friendly offerings. I like to avoid plastic when at all possible. Common plastic items to avoid are drink bottles, candy wrappers, and other packaging materials. Another common item people dispose of is paraffin wax remnants from candles, but they often don't think about the negative environmental impact.

Most of my offerings that end up in nature consist of food items placed at the base of trees or in natural areas sans any wrappers or packaging. I generally place them directly onto the ground and pour any liquids directly onto the earth. Of course I still burn candles; however, I try to burn them down as far as safely possible in an appropriate container. Whatever wax is left over I have been known to save and later melt down to make new candles.

There are some occasions when you may still find a need to make nonbiodegradable and less-earth-friendly offerings. Many of these are often left at indoor or enclosed shrines and may consist of jewelry, trinkets, prayer beads, candles, and other items. One must consider the fact that these will eventually face a "terminal disposal" beyond your leaving them. They will eventually ultimately be removed from said drop-off point. If we ourselves are not tending the site the offering is left at, we must assume that it will end up in the trash. An important realization we must all have is that there is no such thing as "away." Nothing "goes away." Ever. We must think about the fact that we may be contributing to landfills, which we have finite space for. Landfills also have a lifespan before they must be covered over and discontinued, and a new site must be opened up. Landfill sites have extremely limited reuse after being designated as such. So, no matter where you make, deposit, or dispose of your offering, you can see that its material and impact are a pretty substantial concern.

Let's talk a bit about some ecological choices we can make regarding our offerings. A nice, environmentally friendly choice is wildflower seeds. These can be tossed directly into the environment as an offering that also beautifies. Please be careful to choose wildflower seeds native to your geographic location and environment; you do not want to spread invasive species! Biodegradable and beautiful, dried flower petals are another wonderful choice. Choose flowers that energetically align with your purpose. Unwrapped chocolate is another great choice.

Please choose your deposit location carefully; as mentioned earlier, you don't want any wildlife that would be harmed from its consumption getting ahold of it (consider burying it). Any paper materials used to write spells, petitions, or letters or for wrapping an offering should be biodegradable. Such paper is available if you look around online. Another option for the wrapping for offering bundles you'll deposit in nature is a plant leaf with some earth-friendly twine or string. Some traditions dispose of spell bags and gris-gris in the great outdoors. Sadly, the bags are often made of synthetic fibers that may not break down. So leaves, biodegradable paper, and organic fibers offer a better, more environmentally conscious choice.

How should we address materials that are not as earth friendly? The goal is to realize that it will be around for a very long time and try to choose offerings accordingly. Items such as glass candle containers can be reused. If the object can be passed on to another person after a period of time, that is another option. Passing on an offering to someone else can be seen as conferring the blessings of the entity to whom the offering was made—double blessing for your efforts!

Also, before throwing anything away, check for recyclability. Using recyclable materials is another factor to consider. However, if something simply must be thrown away, it's best to do it yourself. While I discourage the needless filling of landfills, it is better than disposing of the item in nature, where less-controlled harm may come from it.

Immaterial Offerings

Something to remember about the materials of our offerings is that perhaps they need not be material at all. The creation of a song, poem, or chant can be just as valid an offering as any. Let the creative muses inspire you and lead you to the creation of something totally unique and power filled. You can use an appropriate existing piece; however, it adds a great deal of potency to go through the effort of developing an original creation. Let the divine inspiration flow!

Another offering idea that is ecological is to tend a houseplant or garden in honor of a deity, spirit, place, or other entity. This can be seen as a long-term offering, as not only are you offering the plant but also your labor of love and service in tending to the plant. Again, if planting outside, be sure to choose noninvasive species. As the plant grows, so will the power of your offering. In fact, prayer trees have a long cross-cultural history. In this scenario, the tree becomes a sacred site and altar all its own, a place where you can make other offerings. As the site is used over time, the power continues to grow. Another benefit: you get to assure that any offerings left there meet a proper and environmentally friendly ending.

Hopefully, after this exploration, you can agree that it does all of us a favor, including our beloved earth, to put more thought into our choice of offering materials. To make an offering is a sacred act of devotion, and, therefore, we want to avoid inadvertently turning it into an act of desecration. May you walk softly upon and receive the blessings of our beloved Mother Earth.

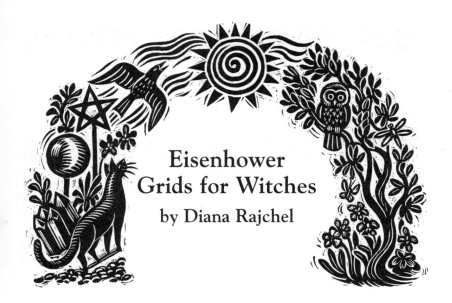

Eisenhower Grids for Witches
by Diana Rajchel

Stereotypes about American Witches have changed since the 1970s—especially when it comes to our organizing skills. Magical people can be straight or gay, wear tie-dye or Armani, join the military or run a chapter of Food Not Bombs, and a few might even join their local Kiwanis Club. Free spirits keep calendars now. Staying on track means that sometimes we need a little help from the nonmagical world.

A particularly powerful practical tool for organizing that many a Witch will love is the Eisenhower Grid. Inspired by United States President Dwight D. Eisenhower, this tool employs the philosophy that "what is important is seldom urgent and what is urgent is seldom important." Decades later, productivity guru Stephen Covey capitalized on this idea by designing a visual tool for sorting critical tasks. Any Witch with a job, family, or to-do list can see the benefits of trimming tasks down to what matters most.

This Eisenhower Grid (also referred to as Covey's time management matrix) categorizes tasks into four slots: important and urgent, important and not urgent, urgent and not important, and not urgent and not important. These categories can change depending on the nature of a project or goal. So, for example, a Witchy household might have a matrix that looks like this:

Important and Urgent	Important and Not Urgent
• Change the cat litter box! (Dear God!) • Rent due • Perform monthly house cleansing/blessing	• Full Moon this weekend—ritual with neighbors • Reschedule hair appointment • Return books to coven brother
Urgent and Not Important	**Not Urgent and Not Important**
• Taco Tuesday coupons almost expired • Sale on black candles at party store • Research winter traditions for the dark half of the year • Laundry	• Rearrange bookshelves by color • See if anyone wants to trade incense • Danny Kaye movie marathon • Check email

Choosing tasks that are deadline dependent (who wants to sit with dirty cat litter for long?) ensures you complete the most important tasks first. If ordered well, finishing a task from the first box serves you the best. When you, like most human beings, don't accomplish everything you set out to in one day, the grid visual makes it clear how much what you did or didn't get done really matters. At the end of each day, you can look at the remaining lists and decide whether to upgrade their importance or to drop them from your plans.

You need not restrict yourself to the language of urgency when mapping your grid. You can adapt the box labels to your lifestyle. Some prefer "do now, do later, delegate." A version meant for chronic overdoers assigns the grid as "need to, want to, do later, appointments." An added benefit, the need to/want to separation gives people a clear, sane, visual way to say no. You may even create multiple priority grids for different projects, or, preferably, delegate one priority grid to each family or project member. If, however, you know you do too much, then stick to one grid.

The goal of this system is to reduce the feeling of task overwhelm. To help you find peace with your to-dos, these practices may help:

Estimate Your Task Time

It helps to add a line next to each item on your grid noting about how much time a task takes. For lower priorities, state how much time you are willing to spend. If you agreed to bring the altar items for your coven's Full Moon ritual, do you have two hours to spend digging through a dollar store? If you have the means, can you order online, finding what you need in fifteen minutes, and then using the saved seventy-five minutes to clean your home altar if that feels more important?

Assume One Grid Equals about One Week

If anyone in the universe completes their to-do list every day, that person lives on a planet besides Earth. These lists don't account for emergencies, opportunities that arise, or situation changes that alter the course and overall purpose of some tasks. If you can only get one thing done in a day, that's okay. If you can't finish one, break down that task into smaller tasks you know you can do. If you see a task within a task that troubles you, you now see exactly where and how to ask for help. For example, if you want to prepare for the family Samhain celebration, it may take up to a week to decide what rituals or traditions you want to honor—and only then are you ready to shop for any holiday supplies.

Drop Items from Your Grid

The point of an Eisenhower Grid isn't to make sure you get all the things done—it's to make sure you complete the most important tasks. You personally don't need to organize your daughter's bake sale, especially if you need that time to see a doctor for that lingering cold. The grid lets you see what really takes greatest priority because the unspoken rule of using it is that you value yourself and your time.

The *Witches' Datebook* Eisenhower Grid

You can adapt prioritization to seasons, astrological events, and Moon cycles for long-range magical planning. So, at the beginning of the year, if you have one or two set goals for where you want to be at the end of the next year, you can use the priority matrix to sort out exactly what and how much magic you want to put towards that goal. It also lets you look at all your workings—requests from friends, emergency castings, short-term problem-solvers—and decide which ones do and don't

move you toward your end-of-year goals.

Long-term goal setting and grid use pairs well with bullet journaling. The wide format of the datebook's daily slots just happens to offer plenty of room to bullet journal. The bullets allow you a "brain dump," and the matrix allows you to sort those into identifiable tasks, placing emphasis on those that best serve your long-term goals. Not only can you see astrological events and major holidays and align tasks with them, you can examine bullet points and fit them into priority boxes. Soon you'll be expert at knowing what to keep and what to drop.

When to Journal and Grid

Popular productivity wisdom suggests that you plan tasks for the next day an hour before you go to bed. If you wish to try this wisdom, make a self-care routine of it. Grab a pleasant beverage, set a timer, and write your points with a favorite colored pen. Spend no more than twenty minutes on this planning routine. Make a note next to each task in the grid about how much time it should take. Factor in time-sucks like traffic, misplaced items, and social media. On larger projects, such as writing books, you will have to prioritize by subtask ("produce five hundred words today") rather than expecting to complete the entire project in one day.

Visual and electronic aids for using the Eisenhower Grid are abundant. Pinterest users have posted many versions of the grid, and a quick search reveals priority grid smartphone apps ranging from free to wildly expensive. You can always draw your own grid on a piece of paper daily. If, after a few weeks of trying out the grid system, you find this method works for you, you can tweak common programs like OneNote and Google Keep for grid use.

Witches are starting to think further into the future than the common magical goals of love and money; what once was love is now a long-term relationship and what once was money is now a retirement plan. Use the grid for achieving those long-range goals in both practical and magical ways. You may decide you want to max out your IRA contribution this year—you might set as an urgent goal first to talk to your credit union about how to do this, and then on the next bullet point plan to research long-term prosperity magic.

The day of the disorganized Pagan has faded from stereotype. Too many Pagans have families, own businesses, and need both spiritual and functional continuity to ensure a happy spiritual practice in the twenty-first century. Fortunately, while many Pagans and Witches were pushing the envelope of spiritual living, Covey and many other productivity experts were discovering ways to get more accomplished in less time and to get more pleasure from the time freed. Just as we often adapt our religious beliefs to make room for scientific discovery, we can learn new ways of planning our lives—the free time obtained this way may seem like magic, or even wealth!

Sources

Baer, Drake. "Dwight Eisenhower Nailed a Major Insight about Productivity." Business Insider. April 10, 2014. http://www.businessinsider.com/dwight-eisenhower-nailed-a-major-insight-about-productivity-2014-4.

Lim, Shawn. "10 Things Most Successful People Do at Night before Sleep." Lifehacker. Accessed June 25, 2017. http://www.lifehack.org/articles/productivity/10-things-most-successful-people-night-before-sleep.html.

Mueller, Steve. "Stephen Covey's Time Management Matrix Explained." Planet of Success. Last modifed April 1, 2017. http://www.planetofsuccess.com/blog/2015/stephen-coveys-time-management-matrix-explained/.

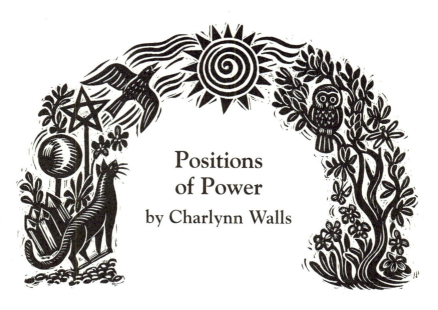

Positions of Power
by Charlynn Walls

In our daily lives, we connect with one another in a variety of ways. We are often able to verbalize what is going on, but we also communicate in nonverbal ways as well. Body posture and gestures communicate a wealth of information to those around us. The same is true in our spiritual practice. We can verbalize our intentions via spoken spells and incantations, but we also convey our intent through our body position and the gestures that we use. Body position and gestures can be an integral part of our daily practices and can impact how we connect with the energies around us. Our bodies can be open or closed and therefore be open to accepting energy into ourselves or withdrawing from it. Incorporating these positions into our daily devotions can help us remain in balance.

Body Position Symbolism

There have been several times over the years when I incorporated the use of body position to enhance my connection and enable me to draw energy from the Sun, Moon, and earth. One reason to utilize a particular body position is to mimic the relational space between the heavenly bodies within the universe. The farther away from the earth the more open the body posture becomes. Likewise, the closer to the earth the more centered the positioning becomes. When the practitioner sets their intention upon a particular task, they can enhance and increase their likelihood of success by consciously choosing how to hold their body in a similar way.

Connecting with the Sun, Moon, and Earth

There are many simple things we can do on a daily basis that can deepen our connection with the energies around us. For instance, it is important to start the day off on the right foot. When I have been feeling particularly stressed and out of sorts, I will often begin my day with the rising of the Sun as a type of meditative exercise. Though, if you are not an early riser, you can do this whenever you wake up as well. It is an excellent way to regain focus on the important matters in your life, and I did this for an extended period of time after the death of my grandmother.

I would greet the Sun and take in its energy by creating an open body posture, which has one reaching toward the Sun's rays as it is farther away from the earth. I extended my arms out from my body with palms up. My feet were positioned about shoulder width apart with my head tilted up. This open posture allows the Sun to illuminate every part of one's being, allowing for the most absorption of solar energy. The Sun fell specifically on my face, hands, and solar plexus. After I welcomed the Sun, I was able to go about my day with renewed energy and spirit.

Many times, in the process of my daily practice I have also sought to work directly with lunar energies. These are energies that I feel pulled to work with on a consistent basis. Though you can work with any phase of the Moon, when utilizing this type of practice, you will want to work through the waxing phase. When I was still very new to the path, I performed an intake of lunar energy to enable me to work with the Goddess in order to see the path I needed to follow.

I went out at the apex of the Full Moon on a beach on the West Coast. When meeting the Moon to work with those energies, I held my body in a slightly more restrained position. My arms were held in toward the body with palms up (or your arms can be crossed over the chest). My feet were positioned just slightly apart, with my face looking up toward the Moon. This position mimics the relationship of the Moon to the earth. At the time, I ran mostly on instinct, but what I

did worked. Since then, I use this in my daily practice any time I seek clarity on my path or when I need to reconnect with my highest self.

The planet we live on is also the one we have the closest connection to. When I began to work earth energies into my daily practice, it began as a ritual give and take. I would receive energy from the earth to center and return energy to the earth as a way of giving thanks.

To connect with the earth and establish a link, I become as close to the ground as possible. This body position is much tighter in comparison to the others. I sit or lie on the ground to increase the connection. When possible, I take off my shoes and dig my toes into the loam or sand and draw up the energy from the earth through the soles of my feet. When giving energy back, I established a connection with my hands in a similar fashion.

In addition to working with planetary energies, you can also utilize these body positions for rituals designed for invoking the Sun, Moon, and earth. They can and have been used in the drawing down of the Moon and Sun. It should be noted that for instances of invocation it is highly recommended to have at least one trusted individual with you to ease the transition back from the altered state of consciousness.

Connection through Gestures

Gestures used in spells and ritual can also be powerful ways to connect with the forces around us. A common way to do this is to face the direction of the quarter being called and raise your hand or hands in salute in a similar manner to reaching out to shake the hand of someone we are meeting. Other ways that we can increase the power behind our rituals and spells is to be mindful of what our intent is and to mirror that through the use of gesture.

When anointing or initiating an individual, we may draw symbols around or on the body of the person we are working with. These can be universal symbols, such as those created for earth, air, fire, or water. They can also be much more personal in nature and have a specific meaning to the individual or group.

Another way to increase the power of a ritual space is to use a gesture once the quarter has been called. I have often used the invoking pentagram to open each quarter and banishing pentagrams to close a quarter. It is particularly effective when the final gesture of "drawing" the pentagram is completed with the final words spoken at that quarter.

When working to raise energy, individuals or groups will often conduct a spiral dance to show the energy how to flow within the circle. Similarly, you can gather the energy within the circle and direct it with your arm, athame, or wand, starting far out from the body and bringing it spiraling in with the apex being achieved as the item is pointing directly above the head of the individual. This gesture works well for small, confined spaces and achieves the same result as a spiral dance. It also alleviates the worry of tripping over one's own feet!

There are other motions that can be utilized in spells or rituals to represent our intentions. I have also employed the use of other hand gestures. When working on banishings, I visualize what I want to be rid of and push it away with my hands. I begin as close to my body as possible and then move my hands outward until I reach my limit. Then I repeat the motion until the spell is complete. Sometimes, I emphasize the removal of any residual energy by flicking my fingers and shaking my hands after the last push.

If I am in a place where it is unsafe to leave a candle burning, I will often extinguish the one in the physical plane while holding the flame that is to continue burning on the astral plane. While I see this in my mind's eye, I am also completing that intention by holding the astral flame as if to protect it and in order to set it aside.

When working with others, gestures can also be an extremely powerful tool. Some of the most powerful rituals for me were conducted by people who knew the importance of using gesture. Their use can direct or regain a group's focus.

Conclusions

There are limitless possibilities when utilizing body positioning and gestures to enhance magickal practice. Words are powerful, and they have the ability to inspire. Actions, however, tell a story that words alone cannot. They convey the depth of our grief, love, and devotion. We have to consciously decide what body position and gestures to utilize. When we do so with purposeful intent in order to convey the same meaning as our words, we can increase the power behind our spells and rituals.

January 2019

S	M	T	W
		1	2
6	7	8	9
13	☽	15	16
20	☺	22	23
☾	28	29	30
3	4	5	6

T	F	S	
3	4	☽	**Notes**
10	11	12	
17	18	19	
24	25	26	
31	1	2	
7	8	9	

December/January

31 Monday
4th ♏
♂ enters ♈ 9:20 pm
Color: White

New Year's Eve

1 Tuesday
4th ♏
☽ v/c 5:26 pm
Color: Scarlet

New Year's Day
Kwanzaa ends

2 Wednesday
4th ♏
☽ enters ♐ 3:58 am
Color: Brown

3 Thursday
4th ♐
Color: White

For meditation, wear sapphire or sodalite.

4 Friday
4th ♐
☽ v/c 12:41 pm
☽ enters ♑ 1:55 pm
☿ enters ♑ 10:40 pm
Color: Coral

30   *Set in Eastern Standard Time (EST)*

The Witch's Jewelry

A Witch's jewelry is probably one of the most personal magical tools; after all, we wear jewelry on our body within our energy field for long periods of time. When worn, certain metals, symbols, and stones can enhance your personal energy in different ways. Jewelry can also be part of a spell. A necklace, ring, or bracelet can be enchanted for many different magical purposes and worn daily. Some Witches wear jewelry with magical symbols or a particular god, goddess, or spirit guide in order to carry that energy with them. I love wearing pieces of magical jewelry to serve as a constant reminder of my commitment to my spiritual path. Some Witches have special jewelry they only wear during ritual, some even wear bejeweled headpieces. I know Witches who wear necklaces of traditional amber and jet either earned through the ranks in their covens or crafted themselves. One of my favorite forms of magical jewelry is a bracelet or anklet made from embroidery floss either as macramé or braided with stone and glass beads. I create these while focusing on my magical intention; I tie it on and wear it all the time.

—Mickie Mueller

☽ Saturday
4th ♑
New Moon 8:28 pm
Color: Black

Solar eclipse 8:28 pm, 15° ♑ 25'

6 Sunday
1st ♑
☿ D 3:27 pm
Color: Gold

Set in Eastern Standard Time (EST)

January

7 Monday
1st ♑
☽ v/c 1:20 am
☽ enters ♒ 1:46 am
♀ enters ♐ 6:18 am
Color: Lavender

8 Tuesday
1st ♒
Color: Red

Red focuses on survival, courage, sexuality, competition, and fire.

9 Wednesday
1st ♒
☽ v/c 11:53 am
☽ enters ♓ 2:44 pm
Color: White

Eucalyptus incense brings clarity and healing.

10 Thursday
1st ♓
Color: Purple

11 Friday
1st ♓
☽ v/c 9:25 am
Color: Pink

Set in Eastern Standard Time (EST)

Basil and Lemon Fish Cakes

½ cup fresh basil, minced
Zest of 1 lemon
⅔ cup lemon juice
½ cup smoked sardines, minced
½ cup herring in lemon, minced
1½ cup garbanzo flour
1½ cup wheat flour
1 tsp. baking powder
½ tsp. baking soda
½ tsp. Atlantic sea salt
2 egg yolks
1 cup of Greek yogurt

Mix everything together in a medium-size bowl. On medium-high heat bring 3 T. safflower oil to 350°F. Fry the balls by scooping 1 tsp. at a time into the oil. Fish out when golden brown and keep warm in a 200°F oven until serving. Balls are best served on skewers 3 or 4 at a time. Garnish with mayonnaise and lemon juice, and then enjoy piping hot! Makes 6–12 cakes.

Trying new foods for the New Year is not always easy; like all feckless acts of blind trust, it takes the gusto of wild abandon. Some Mediterranean flavors are iconic of romance by the sheer glory of their exotic and fearless ingredients. The epicurean rewards of life, after all, are refreshingly zesty if not unexpectedly delicious.

—Estha K. V. McNevin

12 Saturday
1st ♓
☽ enters ♈ 3:18 am
Color: Blue

13 Sunday
1st ♈
Color: Yellow

Izumo Taisha in Japan is a Shinto shrine for the kami, *or nature spirits.*

Set in Eastern Standard Time (EST)

January

◐ Monday
1st ♈
2nd quarter 1:46 am
☽ v/c 10:56 am
☽ enters ♉ 1:31 pm
Color: Gray

Iron corresponds to Mars, fire, and masculine energy. Use it to prevail in conflicts.

15 Tuesday
2nd ♉
Color: Black

Hedgehogs teach humility and defense.

16 Wednesday
2nd ♉
☽ v/c 1:34 pm
☽ enters ♊ 8:00 pm
Color: Topaz

17 Thursday
2nd ♊
Color: Crimson

18 Friday
2nd ♊
☽ v/c 8:32 pm
☽ enters ♋ 10:44 pm
Color: Coral

Set in Eastern Standard Time (EST)

19 Saturday
2nd ♋
Color: Indigo

When your ear itches, someone is talking about you.

20 Sunday
2nd ♋
☉ enters ♒ 4:00 am
☽ v/c 8:50 pm
☽ enters ♌ 10:54 pm
Color: Orange

Sun enters Aquarius

January

☺ Monday
2nd ♌
Full Moon 12:16 am
Color: White

Martin Luther King Jr. Day
Celtic Tree Month of Rowan begins
Cold Moon
Lunar eclipse 12:16 am, 0° ♌ 52'

22 Tuesday
3rd ♌
☽ v/c 8:19 pm
☽ enters ♍ 10:22 pm
Color: Maroon

*"Only in the darkness can you see
the stars."* —Martin Luther King Jr.

23 Wednesday
3rd ♍
Color: Yellow

24 Thursday
3rd ♍
☿ enters ♒ 12:49 am
☽ v/c 8:50 am
☽ enters ♎ 11:02 pm
Color: Green

Iris grants inspiration and opens the way for divinity.

25 Friday
3rd ♎
♀ enters ♐ 1:08 pm
Color: Purple

Set in Eastern Standard Time (EST)

The Wondrous Moon

Once upon a time there was . . . the Moon! A traditional means of teaching lessons and revealing truths, fairy and folk tales are peopled with heroes and heroines, sometimes in the form of the Moon who appears as both character and catalyst. In her face we see our own, in her shadows, the depths of our personal darkness. Over the course of the year, celebrate Luna's full phase with the wisdom of legend. What does she see as she changes from moment to moment? Hans Christian Andersen might have been pondering this when he penned "What the Moon Saw" in 1840. From her perch in the heavens, the Moon watches over the world and all the people in it. Night after night she reports on the beauty of nature that she sees and revels in the mundane details of people's everyday lives. Her message? There is magic and wonder in all things.

At January's Full Moon, ask Luna to help you see and appreciate the wonders of the world around you, great and small:

> Luna, show me what you see,
> That I, like you, may blessed be.

—Natalie Zaman

26 Saturday
3rd ♎
Color: Gray

Elder is associated with witches and popular for magic wands.

○ Sunday
3rd ♎
☽ v/c 12:21 am
☽ enters ♏ 2:31 am
4th quarter 4:10 pm
Color: Yellow

February 2019

S	M	T	W
3	☽	5	6
10	11	☾	13
17	18	☺	20
24	25	●	27
3	4	5	6

T	F	S	Notes
	1	2	
7	8	9	
14	15	16	
21	22	23	
28	1	2	
7	8	9	

January/February

28 Monday
4th ♏
☽ v/c 5:39 pm
Color: Ivory

Unktome is a Native American trickster who takes the form of a spider.

29 Tuesday
4th ♏
☽ enters ♐ 9:33 am
Color: Gray

30 Wednesday
4th ♐
Color: Brown

31 Thursday
4th ♐
☽ v/c 5:33 pm
☽ enters ♑ 7:47 pm
Color: Turquoise

Turquoise brings about transformation, renewal, invention, and fellowship.

1 Friday
4th ♑
☿ enters ♓ 6:04 am
Color: Pink

Set in Eastern Standard Time (EST)

Imbolc: Summoning the Flame

Yuletide has come and gone. This time of year can feel relatively stagnant for those living in colder climates. The Sun is waxing, but where is he exactly? Is he truly returning? Imbolc occurs near the apex of the zodiac sign Aquarius, which is a sign of uniqueness, art, and mystical creativity. Try organizing a casual artistic gathering. Invite friends, family, and community members to gather for a night of making art. Use your intuition to determine the styles of art you'd like to integrate. These crafts should be focused on a binding theme: light! Contemplate the force of light and what it means in your life. How does the Sun's light align with spiritual and esoteric aspects of your life and in the lives of others? Regardless of the artistic media, be sure that your public gathering (or private observance) focuses on the slow-but-steady return of the Sun. While the Sun's stirring can feel covert—even undetectable—remember that your artistic designs focused on light and life work on a magickal level to harness the Sun's illuminating energy in your own life and in the lives of your friends, family, and community.

—Raven Digitalis

2 Saturday
4th ♑
Color: Blue

Imbolc
Groundhog Day

3 Sunday
4th ♑
☽ v/c 5:53 am
☽ enters ♒ 8:03 am
♀ enters ♑ 5:29 pm
Color: Amber

Imbolc crossquarter day (Sun reaches 15° Aquarius)

Set in Eastern Standard Time (EST)

February

☽ Monday
4th ≈
New Moon 4:04 pm
Color: Silver

5 Tuesday
1st ≈
☽ v/c 6:59 pm
☽ enters ♓ 9:02 pm
Color: Scarlet

Lunar New Year (Pig)

6 Wednesday
1st ♓
Color: Topaz

Jasmine incense promotes wisdom and psychic dreams.

7 Thursday
1st ♓
☽ v/c 5:14 pm
Color: Purple

*Among the water stones are
aquamarine, lapis lazuli, pearl, and selenite.*

8 Friday
1st ♓
☽ enters ♈ 9:34 am
Color: White

9 Saturday
1st ♈
Color: Brown

10 Sunday
1st ♈
☿ enters ♓ 5:51 am
☽ v/c 6:48 pm
☽ enters ♉ 8:28 pm
✸ enters ♊ 11:21 pm
Color: Orange

Tungsten is tough and protective. It makes a good shield for hostile environments.

Set in Eastern Standard Time (EST)

February

11 Monday
1st ♉
Color: Gray

*Lake Titicaca between Peru and Bolivia is said to be
the site where life began, according to local religion.*

☉ Tuesday
1st ♉
☽ v/c 5:26 pm
2nd quarter 5:26 pm
Color: Red

Carry columbine flowers for courage and willpower.

13 Wednesday
2nd ♉
☽ enters ♊ 4:32 am
Color: Brown

14 Thursday
2nd ♊
♂ enters ♉ 5:51 am
Color: Green

Valentine's Day

15 Friday
2nd ♊
☽ v/c 7:48 am
☽ enters ♋ 9:03 am
Color: Rose

Set in Eastern Standard Time (EST)

Blades, Both Practical and Magical

There are several types of blades Witches use for magic; some are used to direct energy with a commanding presence, while others have more practical applications. A knife used strictly for ritual is often referred to as an athame. Traditionally, they are black handled, but that guideline isn't followed by all modern Witches. Many Witches also use a ritual sword in a similar fashion. Some prefer to keep athames and swords dull since they are traditionally not used for cutting. I sometimes cast a circle and call in spirits with a wand, but if I'm doing some big protection magic and need to throw down the gauntlet, I use my athame, the ultimate Witch's weapon, for a totally different vibe in my circle. Another type of blade specifically meant to cut cords in ritual, harvest herbs for magic, incise candles, and other practical tasks is sometimes called a boline and often has a white handle. Kitchen Witches will usually not differentiate between a knife used for casting energy or mundane cutting tasks, deeming every tool in the kitchen sacred for all magical purposes.

—Mickie Mueller

16 Saturday
2nd ♋
Color: Black

Althea incense stimulates psychic senses.

17 Sunday
2nd ♋
☽ v/c 9:17 am
☽ enters ♌ 10:21 am
Color: Yellow

February

18 Monday
2nd ♌
⚷ enters ♈ 4:10 am
♀ ℞ 11:40 am
☉ enters ♓ 6:04 pm
Color: Lavender

Presidents' Day
Celtic Tree Month of Ash begins
Sun enters Pisces

☺ Tuesday
2nd ♌
☽ v/c 8:51 am
☽ enters ♍ 9:47 am
Full Moon 10:54 am
Color: White

Quickening Moon

20 Wednesday
3rd ♍
☽ v/c 8:52 pm
Color: Yellow

21 Thursday
3rd ♍
☽ enters ♎ 9:17 am
Color: Crimson

*Olive trees promote security,
wealth, and fidelity in marriage.*

22 Friday
3rd ♎
Color: Pink

An egg with two yolks means a lucky day.

46   Set in Eastern Standard Time (EST)

The Mirror Moon

Many cultures offer tales of foolish characters who mistake the Moon's reflection for the real thing—but fools are sometimes the wisest among us. A character of Turkish lore (and perhaps a historical wise man), Hodja had a reputation for playing the wise fool. Once upon a time, Hodja looked into the well behind his house and saw the reflection of the Full Moon in its depths. Desperate to save her, he got a hook and a rope and tried to fish her out, only to catch the hook on the wall of the well. He pulled and pulled and toppled backward—and beheld the Full Moon in the sky! He believed that he put her back where she belonged—a foolish notion and a wise one too.

This month we celebrate Imbolc and the goddess Brigid, to whom water is a sacred element and to whom many wells and springs are dedicated. At February's Full Moon, use a bowl of water to capture the Moon's reflection. Bless the water for magical work:

Into this watery looking glass,
Let gentle Luna's powers pass.

—Natalie Zaman

23 Saturday
3rd ♎
☽ v/c 10:11 am
☽ enters ♏ 10:56 am
Color: Gray

24 Sunday
3rd ♏
Color: Gold

Set in Eastern Standard Time (EST) 47

March 2019

S	M	T	W
3	4	5	☽
10	11	12	13
17	18	19	☺
24	25	26	27
31	1	2	3

T	F	S	Notes
	1	2	
7	8	9	
☾	15	16	
21	22	23	
☽	29	30	
4	5	6	

February/March

25 Monday
3rd ♏
☽ v/c 7:14 am
☽ enters ♐ 4:19 pm
Color: White

Mama-Cocha is the Incan sea goddess.
Fishermen and sailors pray to her.

○ Tuesday
3rd ♐
4th quarter 6:28 am
Color: Maroon

27 Wednesday
4th ♐
Color: Brown

28 Thursday
4th ♐
☽ v/c 1:17 am
☽ enters ♑ 1:48 am
Color: White

Among the earth stones are green agate,
brown jasper, malachite, and black tourmaline.

1 Friday
4th ♑
♀ enters ♒ 11:45 am
Color: Coral

50   *Set in Eastern Standard Time (EST)*

The Altar of Spirit

An altar is the magical work space used by Witches to honor their gods and goddesses, celebrate seasonal rituals, and cast their spells. This tool is more than just a work space; it's connected to all realms. Some altars are temporarily set up for a ritual and then disassembled after. I used a temporary altar when I celebrated with my various covens and when I taught a yearlong series of classes at a local shop. I found that one of those three-legged round decorator tables worked great; I could remove the legs for travel and safely store it away when not in use. Some Witches are lucky enough to have a permanent altar in their home for magical use whenever they need it. I've seen people use the top of a dresser, a corner table, or even a wall shelf.

Because the altar is like a special meeting place between you and the spirits you work with, it should be kept clean and not used to toss your keys or coffee mug on . . . unless they're part of your spell, of course. Many Witches keep several altars, sometimes for a specific personal deity or purpose, such as healing or prosperity work.

—Mickie Mueller

2 Saturday

4th ♑
☽ v/c 1:47 pm
☽ enters ♒ 2:06 pm
Color: Indigo

3 Sunday

4th ♒
Color: Yellow

"If we do not maintain justice, justice will not maintain us." —Francis Bacon

Set in Eastern Standard Time (EST)

March

4 Monday
4th ≈
Color: Gray

5 Tuesday
4th ≈
☽ v/c 3:05 am
☽ enters ♓ 3:11 am
☿ ℞ 1:19 pm
Color: Black

Mardi Gras (Fat Tuesday)
Mercury retrograde until March 28

☽ Wednesday
4th ♓
♅ enters ♉ 3:26 am
New Moon 11:04 am
Color: White

Ash Wednesday

7 Thursday
1st ♓
☽ v/c 2:08 pm
☽ enters ♈ 3:27 pm
Color: Turquoise

Yurugu is an African god of chaos and rebellion. He stole the yolk from the cosmic egg.

8 Friday
1st ♈
Color: Purple

52   *Set in Eastern Standard Time (EST)*

9 Saturday
1st ♈
☽ v/c 12:14 pm
Color: Blue

Blue comes with will, patience, communication, truth, organization, and water.

10 Sunday
1st ♈
☽ enters ♉ 3:10 am
Color: Orange

Daylight Saving Time begins at 2 am

Eastern Daylight Time (EDT) begins March 10

March

11 Monday
1st ♉
Color: Silver

Dimste is the Baltic goddess of home and security. She is the guardian of homemakers.

12 Tuesday
1st ♉
☽ v/c 5:31 am
☽ enters ♊ 11:48 am
Color: Red

Daffodils are good for wishing spells and spring altars.

13 Wednesday
1st ♊
Color: Brown

☉ Thursday
1st ♊
2nd quarter 6:27 am
☽ v/c 8:30 am
☽ enters ♋ 5:49 pm
Color: Green

15 Friday
2nd ♋
Color: Rose

Bears relate to the subconscious and healing.

Ostara: The Unveiling of Newness

At the spring equinox we enter the sign of Aries in common tropical astrology. Themes of hope and regeneration permeate ancient and modern perspectives of the spring equinox, visibly carried over in Pagan-based imagery such as bunny rabbits, green grass, and colorful eggs. Try "hatching" your own intentions through intentional magick by making a list of attainable goals for the year that you wish to see manifested. Invite your friends or spiritual community to take part in the activity by distributing pastel papers and colorful markers with which to write their goals. Dim the lights and huddle together under a large blanket with a flashlight. It's time to get cozy together! This ritual activity mirrors the gestation of spring. After giggling subsides, visualize yourselves as gestating seeds or embryotic animals.

All together, start reading off your manifestation lists while you slowly rise together and throw off the blanket with a resounding,

> *Welcome Aries, welcome spring!*
> *These manifestations now come into being!*

—Raven Digitalis

16 Saturday

2nd ♋
☽ v/c 2:03 pm
☽ enters ♌ 8:57 pm
Color: Blue

17 Sunday
2nd ♌
Color: Amber

St. Patrick's Day

March

18 Monday
2nd ♌
☽ v/c 11:19 am
☽ enters ♍ 9:41 pm
Color: Ivory

Celtic Tree Month of Alder begins

19 Tuesday
2nd ♍
Color: Gray

☺ Wednesday
2nd ♍
☽ v/c 11:22 am
☉ enters ♈ 5:58 pm
☽ enters ♎ 9:28 pm
Full Moon 9:43 pm
Color: Yellow

Ostara/Spring Equinox
International Astrology Day
Sun enters Aries
Storm Moon

21 Thursday
3rd ♎
Color: White

Purim (begins at sundown on March 20)

22 Friday
3rd ♎
☽ v/c 2:10 pm
☽ enters ♏ 10:16 pm
Color: Coral

Set in Eastern Daylight Time (EDT)

The Troll Moon

Trolls are creatures of betwixt and between. As magical beings they often cause trouble for humans, but not without great reward: in one traditional Scandinavian tale, a peasant girl had the good hap to be wed to a prince in disguise. Had she been able to keep faith for a year and a day, all would have been well, but she insisted on seeing her lover's face. The prince was whisked away to a castle that lay east of the Sun and west of the Moon, doomed to become the husband of the troll princess who lived there. Of course, our heroine manages to rescue her prince, and through her determination and clever dealings with the troll princess, she achieves her greatest potential. In this tale, the Moon is a compass point that emphasizes the in-betweenness of the girl's place in the world. We've all been in this state of limbo—it's rarely pleasant, but once experienced, it often ushers in a new phase of life. Honor the trolls in your life under March's Full Moon. Remember, those who test us make us stronger:

> Tricks and traps under Troll Moon's gaze,
> Help me to greatness in all ways and always.

—Natalie Zaman

23 Saturday
3rd ♏
Color: Indigo

"Go within every day and find the inner strength so that the world will not blow your candle out." —Katherine Dunham

24 Sunday
3rd ♏
☽ v/c 10:24 pm
Color: Orange

Set in Eastern Daylight Time (EDT)

March

25 Monday
3rd ♏
☽ enters ♐ 2:06 am
Color: White

Gendenwitha is the Iroquois goddess of the morning star. She is beautiful but elusive.

26 Tuesday
3rd ♐
♀ enters ♓ 3:43 pm
☽ v/c 10:37 pm
Color: Scarlet

27 Wednesday
3rd ♐
☽ enters ♑ 10:07 am
Color: Topaz

Violets bring protection, healing, and sleep. They are good for dream pillows.

○ Thursday
3rd ♑
4th quarter 12:10 am
☿ D 9:59 am
Color: Purple

29 Friday
4th ♑
☽ v/c 8:05 pm
☽ enters ♒ 9:46 pm
Color: Pink

Set in Eastern Daylight Time (EDT)

Roasted Garlic and Pepper Pasta Salad

This pasta salad is a "spring forward" dish that boosts your body's immunity to seasonal illness.

2 full bulbs of garlic, cloves peeled
6 sweet peppers, deseeded
½ cup dried apricots
2 large tomatoes
1 cup each Castelvetrano and Kalamata olives, pitted and sliced
1 T. capers
1 yellow squash, cut into large chunks
6 T. extra-virgin olive oil
2 T. honey
3 T. balsamic vinegar
1 T. liquid amino acids (such as Braggs)
3 cups penne pasta, cooked, drained, and chilled overnight

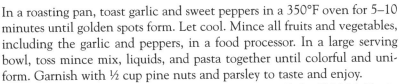

In a roasting pan, toast garlic and sweet peppers in a 350°F oven for 5–10 minutes until golden spots form. Let cool. Mince all fruits and vegetables, including the garlic and peppers, in a food processor. In a large serving bowl, toss mince mix, liquids, and pasta together until colorful and uniform. Garnish with ½ cup pine nuts and parsley to taste and enjoy.

—Estha K. V. McNevin

30 Saturday
4th ≈
Color: Brown

31 Sunday
4th ≈
♂ enters ♊ 2:12 am
☽ v/c 11:02 pm
Color: Gold

Accidentally putting your clothes on backward is a sign of good news.

Set in Eastern Daylight Time (EDT)

April 2019

S	M	T	W
	1	2	3
7	8	9	10
14	15	16	17
21	22	23	24
28	29	30	1
5	6	7	8

T	F	S	Notes
4	☽	6	
11	◐	13	
18	☺	20	
25	◑	27	
2	3	4	
9	10	11	

April

1 Monday
4th ≈
☽ enters ♓ 10:48 am
Color: White

All Fools' Day
April Fools' Day

2 Tuesday
4th ♓
Color: Maroon

Burn honeysuckle incense for
affection, friendship, and happiness.

3 Wednesday
4th ♓
⚷ enters ♈ 11:28 am
☽ v/c 11:36 am
☽ enters ♈ 10:56 pm
Color: Yellow

Use a new broom to sweep good things
into a house, before sweeping dirt out.

4 Thursday
4th ♈
Color: Green

☽ Friday
4th ♈
New Moon 4:50 am
☽ v/c 10:15 pm
Color: Rose

Nethuns is the Etruscan water god.
Ask him for luck in building a new well.

Set in Eastern Daylight Time (EDT)

Broom Parking Only

Witches don't actually ride their brooms, sometimes called besoms, to work, although it would be so cool if we could! A broom is a handy way to cleanse the ritual area or the entire house of astral nasties lurking about. This time-honored tool packs a punch against negative energies. A broom is a symbol of the combination of masculine and feminine energies, so people sometimes jump over a broom at a wedding or handfasting ceremony to symbolize the combining of the household. Years ago one of my covens placed a decorated broom at the edge of our circle and raised it above our heads, opening a doorway to invite initiates into the circle. A decorative broom is an elegant substitution for a wreath on your front door. And where does the image of Witches riding brooms come from? In the old days Pagan rituals of ecstatic dance involved riding a broom hobby horse style around the fire in a shamanic trance of sorts that made participants feel as if they had taken flight. One of my favorite bits of broom folklore is that if your broom falls over and hits the floor, it means that company is coming.

—Mickie Mueller

6 Saturday
1st ♈
☽ enters ♉ 9:06 am
Color: Black

Bees deliver sweetness and communication.

7 Sunday
1st ♉
Color: Gold

April

8 Monday
1st ♉
☽ v/c 4:29 am
☽ enters ♊ 5:15 pm
Color: Gray

9 Tuesday
1st ♊
♀ ℞ 12:35 am
Color: Red

For courage, wear amethyst or tiger's eye.

10 Wednesday
1st ♊
♃ ℞ 1:01 pm
☽ v/c 1:27 pm
☽ enters ♋ 11:31 pm
Color: Brown

Uluru in Australia has pictographs linked with the Dreamtime.

11 Thursday
1st ♋
Color: Crimson

○ Friday

1st ♋
2nd quarter 3:06 pm
☽ v/c 7:33 pm
Color: Pink

White clouds in a clear sky indicate happy times.

Set in Eastern Daylight Time (EDT)

13 Saturday
2nd ♋
☽ enters ♌ 3:50 am
Color: Blue

14 Sunday
2nd ♌
☽ v/c 9:38 pm
Color: Amber

Palm Sunday

Set in Eastern Daylight Time (EDT)

April

15 Monday
2nd ☊
☽ enters ♍ 6:14 am
Color: Ivory

Celtic Tree Month of Willow begins

16 Tuesday
2nd ♍
Color: White

*Roses deal in relationships: red for romance,
pink for friendship, and white for platonic love.*

17 Wednesday
2nd ♍
☽ v/c 12:29 am
☿ enters ♈ 2:01 am
☽ enters ♎ 7:22 am
Color: Topaz

18 Thursday
2nd ♎
Color: Purple

☺ Friday
2nd ♎
☽ v/c 7:12 am
Full Moon 7:12 am
☽ enters ♏ 8:41 am
Color: Coral

Good Friday
Wind Moon

Set in Eastern Daylight Time (EDT)

The Friendship Moon

What will we not do for our dear friends? Once upon a time, Sun and Moon, husband and wife, invited their friend Water to stay with them in their very large house. Alas, their home was not big enough! Water and his creatures quickly filled the house and spilled into the surrounding gardens. Sun and Moon had nowhere to go but . . . up! This is why Sun and Moon live in the sky.

The element of water, so prevalent in spring, is closely connected to emotions. April's Full Moon is a wonderful time to meditate on friendship. To whom are you most closely connected? What do you do for each other? Set out a receptacle (house) under the Full Moon and place a moonstone and a sunstone inside it. Fill the house with water and bless the pair of stones, an amulet for friendship:

To the Moon and back again,
For you, dear friend, anything.

Keep the stone that resonates with you, and give the other to a beloved friend.

—Natalie Zaman

---

20 Saturday
3rd ♏
☉ enters ♉ 4:55 am
♀ enters ♈ 12:11 pm
⚹ enters ♋ 12:38 pm
Color: Brown

Passover begins (at sundown on April 19)
Sun enters Taurus

---

21 Sunday
3rd ♏
☽ v/c 12:00 am
☽ enters ♐ 11:59 am
Color: Orange

Easter

Set in Eastern Daylight Time (EDT)

April

22 Monday
3rd ♐
Color: Silver

Earth Day

23 Tuesday
3rd ♐
☽ v/c 7:44
☽ enters ♑ 6:50 pm
Color: Gray

Cedar relates to the element of earth and grants self-control.

24 Wednesday
3rd ♑
♀ ℞ 2:48 pm
Color: Yellow

25 Thursday
3rd ♑
☽ v/c 3:48 pm
Color: Purple

Almond wood is good for divination and clairvoyance.

○ Friday
3rd ♑
☽ enters ♒ 5:27 am
4th quarter 6:18 pm
Color: White

Orthodox Good Friday

Set in Eastern Daylight Time (EDT)

The Wand of the Witch

A wand is an extension of the Witch who wields it. Wands have a way of directing magical energy that is elegant and diplomatic. They are tools of careful communication and a way to focus energy during ritual or spellwork. You can use a simple branch roughly crafted, an elegantly carved wand with crystals and magical symbols, or anything in between.

If making a wand, you should learn the folklore of the trees that you might want to use wood from, making sure it works well with the kind of magic you want to perform with it. A small branch should only be carefully harvested from a tree after asking permission from the tree's spirit and feeling a positive response in your heart. Only harvest wood for a wand in a way that will not harm the tree. Found wood is another option. You can ask your guides to place the right wand for you in your path. Keep your eyes and your heart open until you find it. Wands can also be made of metal or stone, and I know a Witch who crafted lovely copper and crystal wands that were very powerful.

—Mickie Mueller

27 Saturday
4th ≈
Color: Indigo

Passover ends

28 Sunday
4th ≈
☽ v/c 5:44 am
☽ enters ♓ 6:11 pm
Color: Yellow

Orthodox Easter

Set in Eastern Daylight Time (EDT)

May 2019

S	M	T	W
			1
5	6	7	8
12	13	14	15
19	20	21	22
☾	27	28	29
2	3	4	5

T	F	S	Notes
2	3	☽	
9	10	☾	
16	17	☺	
23	24	25	
30	31	1	
6	7	8	

April/May

29 Monday
4th ♓
♄ ℞ 8:54 pm
Color: Lavender

Hibiscus empowers feminine sexuality and creation.

30 Tuesday
4th ♓
☽ v/c 5:57 pm
Color: Black

Birrahgnooloo is an Australian fertility goddess. She also presides over floods.

1 Wednesday
4th ♓
☽ enters ♈ 6:24 am
Color: White

Beltane/May Day

2 Thursday
4th ♈
Color: Crimson

Frogs represent good luck and fertility for their many eggs.

3 Friday
4th ♈
☽ v/c 4:47 am
☽ enters ♉ 4:18 pm
Color: Pink

Beltane: Magickal May Day Baskets

The energy of Beltane is a direct link to the Upperworld and its associated realms, such as the realms of faeries, angels, and spirit guides. This is a time of hope and connecting with others. One of May Day's time-tested traditions is the giving of special baskets or gifts. I remember piecing together special baskets to leave anonymously at the doorsteps of family members, teachers, and family friends as a kid.

Now, as grown-ups (at least in body!), we can integrate fun traditions like these with our magickal work. Gather your friends or fellow crafty practitioners to create May Day baskets for friends, family members, local businesses, and even total strangers. These baskets can be any size—the more you make, the more magick you can spread. To link with energies of the Upperworld, charge and enchant these baskets with the energy of a Beltane ritual. I recommend music, dance, and chanting to help accomplish this. Conclude the ritual by leaving the baskets on the doorsteps of lucky folks whose spirits you'd like to uplift. Don't forget to include a May Day message of kindness and hope!

—Raven Digitalis

Saturday
4th ♉
New Moon 6:45 pm
Color: Blue

5 Sunday

1st ♉
☽ v/c 11:10 am
☽ enters ♊ 11:40 pm
Color: Orange

Cinco de Mayo
Beltane crossquarter day (Sun reaches 15° Taurus)

Set in Eastern Daylight Time (EDT)

May

6 Monday
1st ♊
☿ enters ♉ 2:25 pm
Color: Silver

Ramadan begins

7 Tuesday
1st ♊
☽ v/c 7:50 pm
Color: Gray

"It is time for parents to teach young people early on that in diversity there is beauty and there is strength." —Maya Angelou

8 Wednesday
1st ♊
☽ enters ♋ 5:06 am
Color: Topaz

9 Thursday
1st ♋
☽ v/c 10:06 pm
Color: White

White stands for unity, purification, honesty, innocence, and childhood.

10 Friday
1st ♋
☽ enters ♌ 9:14 am
Color: Rose

Set in Eastern Daylight Time (EDT)

Peach and Pecan Bran Muffins

3 cups pastry flour, sifted
2 cups pecans, crushed
2 cups cane sugar
½ cup bran flour
¼ cup graham wheat flour
1 tsp. salt
2 tsp. baking powder
1 cup melted butter, unsalted
4 eggs, slightly beaten in 2 cups buttermilk
⅔ cup molasses
1 tsp. vanilla extract, mixed with the paste of 1 vanilla bean
12 peaches, halved, to garnish
Golden syrup to garnish

In a large mixing bowl, combine the wet mixture into the dry mixture. Blend until lumpy and scoop into 24 molded paper cups, fitted into a muffin tin. Bake in a 350°F oven for 20–25 minutes. Garnish with a fresh peach half and drizzle each muffin with 1 T. golden syrup. Serve warm and enjoy.

Comfort food is the glue that grips us by the husk: it reminds us this season that other people are an essential component to our own happiness.
—Estha K. V. McNevin

☽ Saturday
1st ♌
2nd quarter 9:12 pm
Color: Indigo

Inguz is a Germanic god of peace. Pray to him for ending strife.

12 Sunday
2nd ♌
☽ v/c 8:24 am
☽ enters ♍ 12:22 pm
Color: Gold

Mother's Day

Set in Eastern Daylight Time (EDT)

May

13 Monday
2nd ♍
Color: Ivory

Celtic Tree Month of Hawthorn begins

14 Tuesday
2nd ♍
☽ v/c 1:19 pm
☽ enters ♎ 2:51 pm
Color: Red

15 Wednesday
2nd ♎
♀ enters ♉ 5:46 am
♂ enters ♋ 11:09 pm
Color: Brown

Mulberry trees touch on knowledge and willpower. Because silkworms feed on mulberry leaves, the wood also controls silk.

16 Thursday
2nd ♎
☽ v/c 5:37 am
☽ enters ♏ 5:26 pm
Color: Green

Galangal incense breaks curses and other malicious influences.

17 Friday
2nd ♏
Color: Pink

The Thoughtful Moon

One evening a long time ago, Sun, Moon, and Wind went to dine with their cousins, Thunder and Lightning. Selfish Sun and Wind brought nothing back for their mother, Star. Moon, however, saved a bit of each dainty dish to share with her. For their thoughtlessness, Sun and Wind were cursed to burn and bite, but the Moon was—and is—celebrated and blessed for her gentle light.

In May we enter the Goddess season with the celebration of Beltane, and for over one hundred years, we've honored her mother aspect (albeit commercially) on the second Sunday of the month, Mother's Day. Gentleness, inner strength, and thoughtfulness are all aspects of the Divine Feminine and embody great power. The Indian tale "How the Sun, Moon, and Wind Went to Dinner" illustrates that a simple gesture can have long-lasting and indelible results. Soak in the soft beams of May's Full Moon with a mantra to honor the mother in all of us:

> Thoughtful, caring Moon above,
> Illumine gentle ways to live.

—Natalie Zaman

☺ **Saturday**
2nd ♏
☽ v/c 5:11 pm
Full Moon 5:11 pm
☽ enters ♐ 9:21 pm
Color: Black

Flower Moon

---

19 Sunday
3rd ♐
Color: Amber

Cats convey balance and grace.

Set in Eastern Daylight Time (EDT)

May

20 Monday
3rd ♐
☽ v/c 1:05 pm
Color: White

Victoria Day (Canada)

21 Tuesday
3rd ♐
☽ enters ♑ 3:56 am
☉ enters ♊ 3:59 am
☿ enters ♊ 6:52 am
Color: Maroon

Sun enters Gemini

22 Wednesday
3rd ♑
☽ v/c 11:58 pm
Color: Yellow

For eloquence, wear celestite or sardonyx.

23 Thursday
3rd ♑
☽ enters ♒ 1:49 pm
Color: Turquoise

Glastonbury Tor in England is associated with faeries and the Goddess.

24 Friday
3rd ♒
Color: Coral

25 Saturday
3rd ♒︎
☽ v/c 8:51 am
Color: Brown

Rain can symbolize cleansing or tears.

○ Sunday
3rd ♒︎
☽ enters ♓︎ 2:08 am
4th quarter 12:34 pm
Color: Gold

Sunflower brings fresh chances, self-actualization, and joy.

June 2019

S	M	T	W
2	☾	4	5
9	☾	11	12
16	☺	18	19
23	24	○	26
30	1	2	3

T	F	S	
		1	**Notes**
	6	7	8
13	14	15	
20	21	22	
27	28	29	
4	5	6	

May/June

27 Monday
4th ♓
Color: Gray

Memorial Day

28 Tuesday
4th ♓
☽ v/c 12:21 am
☽ enters ♈ 2:32 pm
Color: Scarlet

Kavtha is the Etruscan Sun goddess. She represents new beginnings.

29 Wednesday
4th ♈
Color: Topaz

30 Thursday
4th ♈
☽ v/c 11:08 am
☿ D 10:52 pm
Color: Purple

31 Friday
4th ♈
☽ enters ♉ 12:43 am
Color: White

Fig trees grant fertility, energy, and health.

Set in Eastern Daylight Time (EDT)

The Book of Shadows

A book to record your spells, formulas, dreams, or just your own personal thoughts about magic is a personal treasure and often a work in progress for the lifetime of a Witch. Most Witches I know have several Books of Shadows, and so do I. Many begin by filling an ornate blank book with handwritten spells and rituals, lists of herb correspondences, Moon phases, seasonal celebrations, and more. You can even add pressed herbs and magical images, decorating it much like a scrapbook or altered book until it starts to look like a Witchy tome from a movie. I later found that a more practical choice for me was a three-ring binder with sections that allowed for easier organization as well as the ability to move things around and add things as my book grows. There are traditional covens that have initiates hand copy the coven's material into their own book; all that work shows a commitment to learn the tradition. Every coven and learning circle I've been involved with provided printouts of teaching materials and rituals for each gathering. Each printout eventually becomes part of each member's Book of Shadows.

—Mickie Mueller

1 Saturday

4th ♉
☽ v/c 6:53 pm
Color: Gray

Gray brings balance, acceptance, ambiguity, neutrality, and contemplation.

2 Sunday

4th ♉
☽ enters ♊ 7:48 am
Color: Amber

Set in Eastern Daylight Time (EDT)

June

Monday
4th ♊
New Moon 6:02 am
Color: White

4 Tuesday
1st ♊
☽ v/c 11:42 am
☽ enters ♋ 12:17 pm
☿ enters ♋ 4:05 pm
Color: Red

Ramadan ends

5 Wednesday
1st ♋
Color: Brown

Brown relates to animals, hearth and home, food, earth, and stability.

6 Thursday
1st ♋
☽ v/c 10:10 am
☽ enters ♌ 3:16 pm
Color: Green

"If your actions inspire others to dream more, learn more, do more and become more, you are a leader." —John Quincy Adams

7 Friday
1st ♌
Color: Pink

Fand is the ruling goddess of the Celts and the queen of the faeries.

8 Saturday
1st ♌
☽ v/c 5:23 pm
☽ enters ♍ 5:45 pm
♀ enters ♊ 9:37 pm
Color: Blue

9 Sunday
1st ♍
♆ enters ♉ 5:55 am
Color: Yellow

Shavuot (begins at sundown on June 8)

Set in Eastern Daylight Time (EDT)

June

☾ Monday
1st ♍
2nd quarter 1:59 am
☽ v/c 8:01 am
☽ enters ♎ 8:29 pm
Color: Lavender

Celtic Tree Month of Oak begins

11 Tuesday
2nd ♎
Color: Maroon

A butterfly landing on you foretells a guest coming.

12 Wednesday
2nd ♎
☽ v/c 11:15 am
Color: Topaz

13 Thursday
2nd ♎
☽ enters ♏ 12:02 am
Color: Purple

Silver relates to the Moon, water, and the Goddess.
Sterling silver works well in magical applications.

14 Friday
2nd ♏
☽ v/c 3:46 pm
Color: Rose

Flag Day

Set in Eastern Daylight Time (EDT)

The Moon Child

In days of old, a famous warrior chief was born with the mark of the Full Moon on his breast. Though he had two wives, he had no children to whom he could pass his heritage. Eventually, the younger wife bore him a son, but the elder wife plotted to kill the child. Her plans were foiled by the smallest of creatures; a mouse helped hide the baby and brought him back to his family.

The father of the Moon Child bore the mark of the Divine Feminine on his heart, and so both aspects of divinity exist within each other. Consider the approaching summer as a good time to acknowledge the Divine Masculine in the sphere of the Divine Feminine. (We're knee-deep in the Goddess Season, and the Divine Masculine, represented by the Sun, is at his height at Litha.) This month we also enter the sign of Cancer—the Moon Child. Under the auspices of June's Full Moon, honor the father figures in your life with sensitivity and pride:

> *Child under the Moon, of mother and father,*
> *I am your son, I am your daughter.*

—Natalie Zaman

15 Saturday
2nd ♏
☽ enters ♐ 5:03 am
Color: Indigo

Dragon's blood incense conveys courage, power, and male potency.

16 Sunday
2nd ♐
Color: Gold

Father's Day

Set in Eastern Daylight Time (EDT)

June

☽ Monday
2nd ♐
☽ v/c 4:31 am
Full Moon 4:31 am
☽ enters ♑ 12:13 pm
Color: Silver

Strong Sun Moon

18 Tuesday
3rd ♑
Color: Scarlet

19 Wednesday
3rd ♑
☽ v/c 7:19 am
☽ enters ♒ 10:01 pm
Color: Yellow

*Kilauea in Hawaii is the home of the fire goddess
Pele and, unlike many historic sites, is still quite active.*

20 Thursday
3rd ♒
⚹ enters ♌ 10:37 pm
Color: Crimson

21 Friday
3rd ♒
☽ v/c 10:02 am
♆ ℞ 10:36 am
☉ enters ♋ 11:54 am
Color: Purple

Midsummer/Litha/Summer Solstice
Sun enters Cancer

Set in Eastern Daylight Time (EDT)

Midsummer: Solar Protection

At the summer solstice, the Sun enters the sign of Cancer, the crab. Cancer's energy is greatly focused on the house and home. This domestic emphasis might seem paradoxical considering that Midsummer feels very "extroverted" in nature. So why not combine these two energies? This Midsummer, you may wish to invite your Pagan friends to join you in crafting a potion for the purpose of blessing, cleansing, and protecting everyone's homes. Ask participants to bring components for the brew that feel protective. Be sure to include a healthy amount of salt and vinegar, both of which have protective qualities. Suggested herbs include boneset, cayenne, dill, fennel, pepper, juniper, mugwort, and mullein. In a cauldron or on the stovetop, combine your ingredients with enough fresh water for everyone to take home some of the potion in a jar, vial, or spray bottle. While the potion bubbles for a few minutes, create chants for protection. Charge the mixture under the Midsummer Sun, let cool, strain the contents, and distribute the final product to participants so they can sprinkle it in and around their own homes for protection throughout the year.

—Raven Digitalis

22 Saturday
3rd ♒
☽ enters ♓ 10:01 am
Color: Blue

Cowslips promote health and wealth. They also attract faeries.

23 Sunday
3rd ♓
Color: Orange

Set in Eastern Daylight Time (EDT)

June

24 Monday
3rd ♓
☽ v/c 7:10 pm
☽ enters ♈ 10:38 pm
Color: Gray

"Any plan is bad that cannot be changed." —Italian proverb

○ Tuesday
3rd ♈
4th quarter 5:46 am
Color: Black

Owls are associated with wisdom and prophecy.

26 Wednesday
4th ♈
☿ enters ♌ 8:19 pm
Color: White

27 Thursday
4th ♈
☽ v/c 3:51 am
☽ enters ♉ 9:32 am
Color: Green

Among the fire stones are amber, obsidian, ruby, and tiger's eye.

28 Friday
4th ♉
Color: Coral

Set in Eastern Daylight Time (EDT)

Wild Game Mac and Cheese

This hearty casserole can be frozen in tinfoil or a camp pot and then reheated with coals.

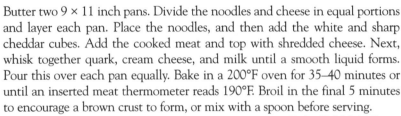

8 cups elbow macaroni, cooked and drained
½ lb. white cheddar, cubed
½ lb. sharp aged cheddar, cubed
1 lb. ground wild game, fully cooked (any wild game; elk is our favorite but lamb, goat, or beef will do)
½ lb. white cheddar, shredded
1 cup quark (crème fraîche)
½ cup soft cream cheese
1 cup whole milk mixed with 3 T. cornstarch stirred into 2 tsp. cold water

Butter two 9 × 11 inch pans. Divide the noodles and cheese in equal portions and layer each pan. Place the noodles, and then add the white and sharp cheddar cubes. Add the cooked meat and top with shredded cheese. Next, whisk together quark, cream cheese, and milk until a smooth liquid forms. Pour this over each pan equally. Bake in a 200°F oven for 35–40 minutes or until an inserted meat thermometer reads 190°F. Broil in the final 5 minutes to encourage a brown crust to form, or mix with a spoon before serving.

—Estha K. V. McNevin

---

29 Saturday
4th ♉
☽ v/c 2:38 pm
☽ enters ♊ 5:09 pm
Color: Black

Black is about wisdom, protection, hex breaking, releasing, and divination.

---

30 Sunday
4th ♊
Color: Yellow

Set in Eastern Daylight Time (EDT)

July 2019

S	M	T	W
	1	2	3
7	8	9	10
14	15	16	17
21	22	23	24
28	29	30	31
4	5	6	7

T	F	S	Notes
4	5	6	
11	12	13	
18	19	20	
25	26	27	
1	2	3	
8	9	10	

July

1 Monday
4th ♊
☽ v/c 5:48 pm
♂ enters ♌ 7:19 pm
☽ enters ♋ 9:24 pm
Color: Ivory

Canada Day

☽ Tuesday
4th ♋
New Moon 3:16 pm
Color: Maroon

Solar eclipse 3:16 pm, 10° ♋ 38'

3 Wednesday
1st ♋
☽ v/c 10:25 am
♀ enters ♋ 11:18 am
☽ enters ♌ 11:19 pm
Color: Yellow

Gold relates to the Sun, fire, and the God.
Pure gold is better for magical working than alloys.

4 Thursday
1st ♌
Color: White

Independence Day

5 Friday
1st ♌
☽ v/c 2:24 am
Color: Purple

Set in Eastern Daylight Time (EDT)

6 Saturday
1st ♌
☽ enters ♍ 12:25 am
Color: Gray

Eagles provide vision and oversight.

7 Sunday
1st ♍
☽ v/c 12:50 pm
☿ ℞ 7:14 pm
Color: Amber

Mercury retrograde until July 31

Set in Eastern Daylight Time (EDT)

July

8 Monday
1st ♍
☽ enters ♎ 2:07 am
⚷ ℞ 7:40 pm
Color: Silver

Celtic Tree Month of Holly begins

○ Tuesday
1st ♎
2nd quarter 6:55 am
☽ v/c 3:36 pm
Color: Red

10 Wednesday
2nd ♎
☽ enters ♏ 5:29 am
Color: Brown

Chromium is radiant and reflective. It makes an excellent mirror shield for returning negative influences to their source.

11 Thursday
2nd ♏
☽ v/c 8:28 pm
Color: Turquoise

12 Friday
2nd ♏
☽ enters ♐ 11:05 am
Color: Pink

Burn copal for protection, purification, or exorcism.

Set in Eastern Daylight Time (EDT)

The Witch in the Mirror

Throughout time, mirrors have been thought of as a tool that bridges a portal between the worlds of the material and the spiritual. Many Witches immediately think of the classic black Witch's mirror made from a piece of clear glass with black paint on the back. These special mirrors are used for scrying, a technique for viewing visions psychically. Usually, the black mirror is set up in a dark room so that there is no reflection on its surface, and the Witch gazes deeply into it while focusing on the question at hand.

Silver reflective mirrors can be magical tools as well. Mirrors can be used on the altar to double your spellwork, and many Witches place a candle on a mirror as part of an uncrossing ritual. Mirrors can also be a tool for reflecting negative energies away from you. Place small mirrors in the window facing out to keep baneful vibes away from your home, or wear mirrored jewelry known as a *hexenspiegel* to reflect and return psychic darts back to the sender. A mirror can be magically empowered to bless and protect you by radiating light and grace throughout your Witchy home.

—Mickie Mueller

13 Saturday
2nd ♐
☽ v/c 9:30 pm
Color: Blue

The Stein Valley in Canada is a traditional location for vision quests, bearing old paintings of visions received there.

14 Sunday
2nd ♐
☽ enters ♑ 7:05 pm
Color: Gold

July

15 Monday
2nd ♑
Color: White

☺ Tuesday
2nd ♑
☽ v/c 5:38 pm
Full Moon 5:38 pm
Color: Black

Blessing Moon
Lunar eclipse 5:38 pm, 24° ♑ 04'

17 Wednesday
3rd ♑
☽ enters ♒ 5:19 am
♀ D 3:06 pm
Color: Topaz

For longevity, wear fossil, petrified wood, or jade.

18 Thursday
3rd ♒
☽ v/c 11:53 am
Color: Purple

19 Friday
3rd ♒
☿ enters ♋ 3:06 am
☽ enters ♓ 5:19 pm
Color: Rose

Wati-Kutjara is an Australian plant god. He takes the form of a lizard.

Set in Eastern Daylight Time (EDT)

The Firefly Moon

Once upon a time there was an elderly couple who longed for a baby. The Lady of the Moon pitied them and sent her daughter, Princess Moon Beam, to them to be their child. The princess grew into a beautiful woman and had many suitors, including the emperor, but she was the Moon Maiden, and so a mortal bride she could not be. On the day she returned to her true mother, she gave the emperor an immortality potion, but rather than live without her, he took it to the highest point in the land—Mount Fuji—and burned it, where it still burns to this day. The Moon Maiden shed tears of light for her adopted parents and her beloved; you can see them every summer in the fireflies that dance the night away, looking for love.

Who is your soul mate? Your best friend? Celebrate the special relationships in your life at July's Full Moon. Like the Moon, fireflies light up the night. If you can, stand among them and ask for a blessing:

By the glow of the Moon and tears of light,
Moon Maiden, bless those who share my life.

—Natalie Zaman

20 Saturday
3rd ♓
Color: Indigo

Benzoin incense releases grief,
anxiety, anger, and other negative feelings.

21 Sunday
3rd ♓
Color: Amber

July

22 Monday
3rd ♓
☽ v/c 4:34 am
☽ enters ♈ 6:02 am
☉ enters ♌ 10:50 pm
Color: Lavender

Sun enters Leo

23 Tuesday
3rd ♈
Color: Scarlet

Copper corresponds to Venus, water, and feminine energy. It aids relationships.

◐ Wednesday
3rd ♈
☽ v/c 10:48 am
☽ enters ♉ 5:42 pm
4th quarter 9:18 pm
Color: Brown

25 Thursday
4th ♉
Color: Crimson

"Exaggeration is truth that has lost its temper." —Kahlil Gibran

26 Friday
4th ♉
Color: Purple

Set in Eastern Daylight Time (EDT)

A Witch's Bell Rings True

A bell in ritual is a call to attention: when you hear it ring, something is about to happen! Bells have been used to clear energy with their ringing vibration throughout the ages and in many varied spiritual paths, including Witchcraft. Some rituals will call for the ring of a bell during different parts of the ritual, often when calling in spirits or to mark the beginning and end of a ceremony. When a bell is rung during ritual, I have always noticed a shift in the energy. Not just for formal circles, chimes or bells hung on front doors keep negative vibrations from entering. When I'm doing a long-term spell that I intend to send energy to daily, I use a bell to awaken the energy and shift into magic mode quickly. I own a little brass bell and a glass one, but my favorite is my Tibetan tingsha chimes. They produce a beautiful lingering tone when struck together. Bells are great for clearing negative energies from an area. A bell produces sound waves that can fill a room in a way that sprinkling blessed water or even smudging with smoke just can't match.

—Mickie Mueller

27 Saturday
4th ♉
☽ v/c 12:28 am
☽ enters ♊ 2:29 am
♀ enters ♌ 9:54 pm
Color: Black

28 Sunday
4th ♊
☽ v/c 11:24 am
Color: Yellow

Dolphins swimming near a ship predict fair seas.

Set in Eastern Daylight Time (EDT)

August 2019

S	M	T	W
4	5	6	☾
11	12	13	14
18	19	20	21
25	26	27	28
1	2	3	4

T	F	S	
1	2	3	**Notes**
8	9	10	
☻	16	17	
22	◐	24	
29	☾	31	
5	6	7	

July/August

29 Monday
4th ♊
☽ enters ♋ 7:31 am
Color: Gray

Chicomeccatl is the Aztec goddess of corn. Pray to her for abundant harvests.

30 Tuesday
4th ♋
☽ v/c 11:32 pm
Color: White

☽ Wednesday
4th ♋
☽ enters ♌ 9:18 am
New Moon 11:12 pm
☿ D 11:58 pm
Color: Yellow

"As she has planted, so does she harvest; such is the field of karma." —Sri Guru Granth Sahib

1 Thursday
1st ♌
☽ v/c 4:48 pm
Color: Turquoise

Lammas/Lughnasadh

2 Friday
1st ♌
☽ enters ♍ 9:20 am
Color: Rose

Lammas: Honoring the Social Harvest

Congratulations, you've made it halfway through the summer! Summertime is a notoriously exhausting time of year for people who work with the land. In many parts of the world, this is the short window of time for tending to the crops and encouraging the harvest. Lammas marks the "first harvest" in the Wheel of the Year. Whether or not you directly work with the earth through gardening or agriculture, we are all social creatures, so it's also important to pay attention to our life's "social harvest." This Lammas, connect with your best friends and closest family members. Reflect on the ways you have fine-tuned your social circle to those with whom you feel perfect love and perfect trust. Consider ways you can encourage more of this energy in your life, such as expanding your social circle and meeting more like-minded souls. Incorporate gratitude into your magick by lighting an orange candle. Meditate. Invite your spiritual guides while you focus on the positive, beautiful, and uplifting aspects of social interaction. Do not only speak aloud your gratitude for those in your sphere, but also affirm wishes for a positive ongoing social harvest.

—Raven Digitalis

---

3 Saturday
1st ♍
Color: Blue

---

4 Sunday
1st ♍
☽ v/c 12:27 am
☽ enters ♎ 9:30 am
Color: Orange

Buttercup enhances self-worth and enables you to choose the right words.

Set in Eastern Daylight Time (EDT)

August

5 Monday
1st ♎
Color: Lavender

Celtic Tree Month of Hazel begins

6 Tuesday
1st ♎
☽ v/c 3:36 am
☽ enters ♏ 11:31 am
Color: Red

A red sunset means fair weather, while a red sunrise means stormy weather.

○ Wednesday
1st ♏
2nd quarter 1:31 pm
Color: White

Lammas crossquarter day (Sun reaches 15° Leo)

8 Thursday
2nd ♏
☽ v/c 10:58 am
☽ enters ♐ 4:35 pm
Color: Green

9 Friday
2nd ♐
Color: Pink

Set in Eastern Daylight Time (EDT)

10 Saturday
2nd ♐
☽ v/c 3:50 pm
Color: Brown

11 Sunday
2nd ♐
☽ enters ♑ 12:50 am
♃ D 9:37 am
☿ enters ♌ 3:46 pm
♅ ℞ 10:27 pm
Color: Yellow

August

12 Monday
2nd ♑
☽ v/c 6:11 pm
Color: Ivory

Use gardenia flowers for emotional first aid.

13 Tuesday
2nd ♑
☽ enters ♒ 11:35 am
Color: Maroon

If you see a shooting star, you may make a wish.

14 Wednesday
2nd ♒
Color: Yellow

☻ Thursday
2nd ♒
Full Moon 8:29 am
☽ v/c 9:02 pm
☽ enters ♓ 11:49 pm
Color: Crimson

Corn Moon

16 Friday
3rd ♓
Color: White

Burn lavender incense for sleep and peace.

Set in Eastern Daylight Time (EDT)

The Restful Moon

Once there was a man who went out to gather firewood on the Sabbath Day, even though he didn't need it. While in the forest, even the animals ran from him, as they knew he should not have been working. He came upon a stranger who asked him why he refused to keep the Sabbath, to which he answered that all days were the same to him. The stranger, an angel in disguise, sent the man to the Moon, where all days are Mondays with no day of rest. Look closely at the Moon—he can still be seen, carrying his bundle!

Rest is important in any spiritual path. It refreshes and restores balance, giving one the ability to continue magical and mundane efforts to the greatest effect. It is a necessity rather than a luxury, particularly at this time of year when the summer heat and the work of the impending harvests take their toll. Set out a chair or blanket under August's Full Moon. Breathe deeply and relax under its restful glow with a simple meditation:

Restful Moon, restore, refresh,
That I may be my very best.

—Natalie Zaman

17 Saturday

3rd ♓
☾ v/c 6:35 pm
Color: Gray

18 Sunday

3rd ♓
♂ enters ♍ 1:18 am
☾ enters ♈ 12:33 pm
Color: Gold

Gold corresponds with fortune,
abundance, justice, the Sun, and the God.

Set in Eastern Daylight Time (EDT)

August

19 Monday
3rd ♈
Color: Silver

20 Tuesday
3rd ♈
Color: Scarlet

Otters are playful and helpful, good friends in a crisis.

21 Wednesday
3rd ♈
☽ v/c 12:06 am
☽ enters ♉ 12:37 am
♀ enters ♍ 5:06 am
Color: Brown

Bismuth forms complex rainbow-colored crystals. It greatly enhances technomagic.

22 Thursday
3rd ♉
☽ v/c 5:33 pm
Color: Turquoise

○ Friday
3rd ♉
☉ enters ♍ 6:02 am
☽ enters ♊ 10:34 am
4th quarter 10:56 am
⚥ enters ♍ 8:00 pm
Color: Rose

Sun enters Virgo

Set in Eastern Daylight Time (EDT)

Ramen Revival Salad

American-Asian salads, all the rage in the 1980s, were a florescent feature of my childhood. This fusion dish remains one of my mom's summer favorites.

2 stalks of celery, julienned
3 carrots, julienned
3 parsnips, julienned
1 small zucchini, julienned
1 turnip, julienned
2 small English cucumbers, diced
6 green onions, sliced at angle into ¹⁄₁₆-inch pieces
6 sweet peppers, cored and julienned
3 cups green cabbage, shredded
3 cups red cabbage, shredded
1 cup pan-toasted sesame seeds
¼ cup rice wine vinegar
4 T. sesame seed oil
2 T. mustard oil
4 T. soy sauce
½ tsp. minced ginger
2 T. raw cane sugar syrup

Toss ingredients together in a large bowl. Let rest for 20 minutes until the vegetables have taken on the flavor of the marinade. Garnish with 6 packs ramen noodles (discard seasoning packet) just before serving so that the top layer is crunchy. Yields 15–20 servings.

—Estha K. V. McNevin

24 Saturday
4th ♊
Color: Black

Hazel corresponds to the element of air and grants wisdom. It also aids in reconciliation.

25 Sunday
4th ♊
☽ v/c 2:58 am
☽ enters ♋ 5:05 pm
Color: Gold

August/September

26 Monday
4th ♋
♀ enters ♏ 4:56 am
Color: Ivory

The Temple of the Sun and the Temple of the Moon at Teotihuacan in Mexico are connected by the Avenue of the Dead.

27 Tuesday
4th ♋
☽ v/c 4:55 am
☽ enters ♌ 7:53 pm
Color: Gray

28 Wednesday
4th ♌
☽ v/c 8:07 pm
Color: Topaz

For peace, wear coral, lepidolite, or blue tourmaline.

29 Thursday
4th ♌
☿ enters ♍ 3:48 am
☽ enters ♍ 7:57 pm
Color: Purple

Rabbits stand for speed and fecundity.

☽ Friday
4th ♍
New Moon 6:37 am
Color: White

Set in Eastern Daylight Time (EDT)

31 Saturday
1st ♍
☽ v/c 4:46 am
☽ enters ♎ 7:08 pm
Color: Indigo

Islamic New Year

1 Sunday
1st ♎
Color: Amber

September 2019

S	M	T	W
1	2	3	4
8	9	10	11
15	16	17	18
22	23	24	25
29	30	1	2
6	7	8	9

T	F	S	Notes
☽	6	7	
12	13	☺	
19	20	☾	
26	27	☽	
3	4	5	
10	11	12	

September

2 Monday
1st ♎
☽ v/c 4:34 am
☽ enters ♏ 7:35 pm
Color: White

Labor Day
Labour Day (Canada)
Celtic Tree Month of Vine begins

3 Tuesday
1st ♏
Color: Black

*Rowan is linked with fire.
It offers protection and strength.*

4 Wednesday
1st ♏
☽ v/c 6:58 am
☽ enters ♐ 11:08 pm
Color: Yellow

☽ Thursday
1st ♐
2nd quarter 11:10 pm
Color: Crimson

6 Friday
2nd ♐
☽ v/c 12:03 pm
Color: Coral

*Pekko is the Finnish god of agriculture. He protects
the growing crops and has a fondness for beer.*

Set in Eastern Daylight Time (EDT)

The Pentacle or Altar Tile

An altar tile or pentacle is a symbol of power and protection placed on the altar. Usually disk shaped, it often bears the magical symbol of the pentagram, but some practitioners use other symbols, such as a triple moon, triquetra, and others, depending on the magical style of the Witch using it. I use mine to bless and charge items such as jewelry, charms, stones, and amulets during ritual. I usually bless each item with water, pass it through smoke for air and over a candle for fire, and then rest it upon my altar tile for the element of earth, allowing it to remain there for the rest of the ritual to soak up power like a magical battery charger. Some people claim that traditional British Witches used pentacles made of wax. If in danger of discovery, the item could be chucked into the hearth fire and would be gone quickly. Modern Witches have altar tiles made of stone, wood, ceramics, or even metal. Ornate altar tiles can be purchased in metaphysical shops, or if you're a crafty Witch, you can make your own using a ceramic tile and ceramic oven-cured paint or a wooden disk and a wood burner.

—Mickie Mueller

7 Saturday
2nd ♐
☽ enters ♑ 6:37 am
Color: Blue

8 Sunday
2nd ♑
Color: Yellow

Set in Eastern Daylight Time (EDT)

September

9 Monday
2nd ♑
☽ v/c 4:30 am
☽ enters ♒ 5:24 pm
Color: Gray

10 Tuesday
2nd ♒
Color: Scarlet

Burn poppyseed for female potency and affection.

11 Wednesday
2nd ♒
☽ v/c 1:22 am
Color: Brown

12 Thursday
2nd ♒
☽ enters ♓ 5:52 am
Color: Green

If an oak tree drops an acorn on you, then you will have good luck.

13 Friday
2nd ♓
Color: White

Set in Eastern Daylight Time (EDT)

The Generous Moon

Long ago, it was common for the Moon to come down from the sky and walk amongst the people. She was especially fond of an old woman living by herself in a small hut. One year, a great famine ravaged the land, and the Moon sorrowed to see the people suffer. Concerned about the old woman, every day she went to the hut and gave her friend a piece of her own flesh to sustain her. The woman thrived, and the Moon grew smaller until she was only a sliver. When the people discovered what happened, they were angry, for the Moon, they said, belonged to everyone. The Moon, however, insisted what she did was necessary to help her friend survive. Eventually, the famine ended, but the Moon never returned to earth. In the sky she remains, waxing and waning to remind us of the importance of generosity. Sharing bounty is an important aspect of Mabon. But need, as the Moon teaches, can happen at any time. Sharing makes everyone richer. Meditate on this truth under September's Full Moon:

Generous Moon, you shared yourself.
Inspire me to share my wealth.

—Natalie Zaman

☺ **Saturday**
2nd ♓
☽ v/c 12:33 am
Full Moon 12:33 am
☿ enters ♎ 3:14 am
♀ enters ♎ 9:43 am
☽ enters ♈ 6:32 pm
Color: Black

Harvest Moon

15 Sunday
3rd ♈
Color: Gold

For friendship, wear chrysoprase, pink tourmaline, or turquoise.

Set in Eastern Daylight Time (EDT)

September

16 Monday
3rd ♈
☽ v/c 12:03 pm
Color: Silver

Dogs work toward cooperation and loyalty.

17 Tuesday
3rd ♈
☽ enters ♉ 6:31 am
Color: Red

Gallium is a metalloid soft enough to melt at human body temperature. It supports transformative and gender work.

18 Wednesday
3rd ♉
♄ D 4:47 am
Color: Topaz

*Zemepatis is the Baltic earth god.
He is the guardian of farmers.*

19 Thursday
3rd ♉
☽ v/c 9:57 am
☽ enters ♊ 4:58 pm
Color: Turquoise

20 Friday
3rd ♊
Color: Pink

Set in Eastern Daylight Time (EDT)

Maple Sugar Sheet Cake

When this cake is baked, the aroma of the season will fill your home with the sweet wisdom and gentle endurance of the maple tree.

4 cups cake flour
1½ cup maple sugar
⅔ cup fine almond flour
4 tsp. baking soda
2 tsp. baking powder
1 tsp. sea salt
4 eggs
2 cups whole milk
3 T. whipping cream
1⅓ cup ghee (clarified butter)
1 cup organic maple tea

Sift the dry ingredients together and slowly add a mixture of the wet ingredients in thirds until a lumpy batter forms. Divide equally in half and pour out into 2 greased 11 × 17-inch jellyroll cake pans. Be sure to leave room for the cakes to rise. Bake in a 350°F oven for 35–40 minutes or until sponge springs back when tested in the middle. Garnish with butter and maple syrup and serve hot nestled with ice cream.

—Estha K. V. McNevin

☽ Saturday

3rd ♊
☽ v/c 10:41 pm
4th quarter 10:41 pm
Color: Indigo

UN International Day of Peace

22 Sunday

4th ♊
☽ enters ♋ 12:50 am
Color: Orange

Copper is for fertility, passion, business, and the Goddess.

September

23 Monday
4th ♋
☉ enters ♎ 3:50 am
☽ v/c 6:05 pm
⚷ ℞ 11:43 pm
Color: Ivory

Mabon/Fall Equinox
Sun enters Libra

24 Tuesday
4th ♋
☽ enters ♌ 5:19 am
Color: Gray

25 Wednesday
4th ♌
☽ v/c 12:14 pm
Color: White

Lemon trees stand for chastity and neutrality.

26 Thursday
4th ♌
☽ enters ♍ 6:37 am
Color: Purple

27 Friday
4th ♍
☽ v/c 11:58 pm
Color: Rose

Set in Eastern Daylight Time (EDT)

Mabon: Inaugurating the Balance

The Sun enters Libra at the fall equinox. In the zodiac, Libra is the divine scales of balance. A theme of balance permeates the fall equinox from every possible angle. This sabbat also marks the beginning of the dark season. Gather with friends, family, community, or coven to observe the equinox however you see fit. Have fun with activities that encourage balance as a group. For example, research some challenging yoga postures to perform together, invoking the energy of balance into yourselves as you work to physically balance your bodies in various positions. Make this an intentional act of magick, incorporating your own chants, affirmations, and visualizations—and have fun! After the balancing acts, grab a large piece of construction paper and have everyone in the group write or draw personal imbalances on the paper. These should reflect both personal and global hindrances that you would like to see disappear in order to encourage equilibrium of mind, body, and spirit. Burn this paper as a group while chanting,

Hindrances leave, depart, begone; only balance may carry on!

—Raven Digitalis

☽ Saturday
4th ♍
☽ enters ♎ 6:03 am
New Moon 2:26 pm
Color: Blue

Among the air stones are aventurine, mottled jasper, mica, and pumice.

29 Sunday
1st ♎
☽ v/c 10:06 pm
Color: Yellow

Set in Eastern Daylight Time (EDT)

October 2019

S	M	T	W
		1	2
6	7	8	9
☺	14	15	16
20	◐	22	23
☾	28	29	30
3	4	5	6

T	F	S	Notes
3	4	☾	
10	11	12	
17	18	19	
24	25	26	
31	1	2	
7	8	9	

September/October

30 Monday
1st ♎
☽ enters ♏ 5:42 am
Color: Lavender

Rosh Hashanah (begins at sundown on September 29)
Celtic Tree Month of Ivy begins

1 Tuesday
1st ♏
Color: Black

2 Wednesday
1st ♏
☽ v/c 5:46 am
☽ enters ♐ 7:44 am
Color: Brown

3 Thursday
1st ♐
♀ D 2:39 am
☿ enters ♏ 4:14 am
Color: Green

The Great Pyramid of Giza in Egypt uses sacred geometry.

4 Friday
1st ♐
♂ enters ♎ 12:22 am
☽ v/c 3:34 am
☽ enters ♑ 1:43 pm
Color: Pink

Ilmatar is the Finnish air goddess. She helped create the world.

Set in Eastern Daylight Time (EDT)

Fire Burn and Cauldron Bubble

A Witch's cauldron isn't only the stuff of legend; many modern Witches have cauldrons that they treasure and use regularly in spells and ritual. The cauldron represents the womb of the Mother Goddess, a powerful vessel of transformation. Many cauldrons are cast-iron, while others are brass, steel, or even ceramic. I know several Witches who put all their spell elements into a large cauldron to allow a spell candle to burn down, finishing the spell in safety by the fireplace. I often use a small cauldron to burn petitions in, handing my wishes to the Goddess. I also keep a small cast-iron cauldron on top of my art table—I call it my "cauldron of inspiration." When I get an idea for an art or writing project that I don't have time for, I write it down and place it in the cauldron, the perfect magical "backburner" for an idea until I come back around to it. Let's not forget that some cauldrons are useful to actually cook in. Another of my favorite cauldrons is a large ceramic-clad cast-iron pot that belonged to my grandmother; it's my go-to cauldron for making herbal infusions, condensers, and magical brews.

—Mickie Mueller

☽ Saturday
1st ♑
2nd quarter 12:47 pm
Color: Gray

Erzulie-Ge-Rouge is the Caribbean loa of vengeance. She is known for her red eyes.

---

6 Sunday
2nd ♑
☽ v/c 7:25 pm
☽ enters ♒ 11:42 pm
Color: Gold

October

7 Monday
2nd ♒
Color: Silver

*Silver deals with dreams, intuition,
psychic powers, the Moon, and the Goddess.*

8 Tuesday
2nd ♒
♀ enters ♏ 1:06 pm
☽ v/c 2:27 pm
Color: Red

9 Wednesday
2nd ♒
☽ enters ♓ 12:05 pm
Color: Yellow

Yom Kippur (begins at sundown on October 8)

10 Thursday
2nd ♓
Color: White

*Katoylla is the Incan thunder god.
He brings rain in times of drought.*

11 Friday
2nd ♓
☽ v/c 5:55 am
Color: Purple

The Moon Cake

Once upon a time, there were ten suns in the sky. As you can imagine, it was very hot on earth—until the giant Hou Yi shot down nine of the suns with bamboo arrows. As a reward, the gods gave him the elixir of life, warning him only to drink one drop every year to ensure good health and longevity. Unfortunately, Hou Yi's wife was greedy and drank so much of the elixir that she floated to the Moon, where she lives to this day. Every year the gods send her eggs and nuts and lotus flowers to bake for them. This is one story about the origin of moon cakes, enjoyed at this time of the year.

October heralds the arrival of Samhain, when thoughts turn to the spirit world and ancestors. As the legend of the moon cake shows us, immortality is a thing of the spirit world, while longevity and good health (the promise of the elixir when taken properly!) are blessings to ask for as you honor your ancestors, perhaps with a bit of moon cake:

Long life, good health,
My ancestors live within myself!

—Natalie Zaman

12 Saturday
2nd ♓
☽ enters ♈ 12:46 am
Color: Black

"Realize that everything connects to everything else." —Leonardo da Vinci

☺ Sunday
2nd ♈
Full Moon 5:08 pm
☽ v/c 5:59 pm
Color: Yellow

Blood Moon

Set in Eastern Daylight Time (EDT)

October

14 Monday
3rd ♈
☽ enters ♉ 12:24 pm
Color: Ivory

Columbus Day
Indigenous Peoples' Day
Thanksgiving Day (Canada)
Sukkot begins (at sundown on October 13)

15 Tuesday
3rd ♉
Color: Maroon

16 Wednesday
3rd ♉
☽ v/c 4:37 am
☽ enters ♊ 10:30 pm
Color: Topaz

Xolotl is the Aztec god of the dead. He rules the underworld and guides souls there.

17 Thursday
3rd ♊
Color: Turquoise

Lilacs assist in remembering past lives and warding off negative entities.

18 Friday
3rd ♊
☽ v/c 10:14 pm
Color: Coral

Set in Eastern Daylight Time (EDT)

19 Saturday
3rd ♊
☽ enters ♋ 6:43 am
Color: Blue

20 Sunday
3rd ♋
Color: Orange

Sukkot ends

October

☽ Monday
3rd ♋
☽ v/c 8:39 am
4th quarter 8:39 am
☽ enters ♌ 12:29 pm
Color: White

Burn frankincense for spirituality or meditation.

22 Tuesday
4th ♌
Color: Scarlet

23 Wednesday
4th ♌
☽ v/c 5:14 am
☉ enters ♏ 1:20 pm
☽ enters ♍ 3:29 pm
Color: Brown

Sun enters Scorpio

24 Thursday
4th ♍
Color: Purple

25 Friday
4th ♍
☽ v/c 9:00 am
☽ enters ♎ 4:20 pm
Color: Rose

Projective stones include aventurine, diamond, lava, and sunstone.

Sacred Smoke to Sweeten the Air

Whether a simple abalone shell or an elegant silver censer, an incense burner is a tool that can transform your magical space. This tool represents the element of air as it wafts transformational smoke around the room, purifying the area and adjusting vibrations to match your magical goals. Some Witches like stick incense and a simple wooden holder; others like something more decorative. I especially like a box burner with a lid full of holes for just the smoke to escape because it contains the ash and keeps it from going everywhere. There are also lovely brass, copper, or silver censers that sit on a table or hang from chains and allow you to burn natural resin incense on special charcoal disks. Frankincense and dragon's blood resin are two of my favorites to burn on incense charcoal. Clay bowls or shells are another kind of burner used to ritually purify with smoke, usually when burning tightly wrapped bundles of herbs like sage or lavender. Smoke rising from an incense burner or censer can also aid in meditation, house blessing and cleansing, aromatherapy, and even divination, if you take note of shapes in the smoke.

—Mickie Mueller

26 Saturday
4th ♎
Color: Indigo

☽ Sunday
4th ♎
☽ v/c 4:22 am
☽ enters ♏ 4:29 pm
New Moon 11:39 pm
Color: Amber

A cricket in the house brings prosperity.

November 2019

S	M	T	W
3	◐	5	6
10	11	☺	13
17	18	◑	20
24	25	☽	27
1	2	3	4

T	F	S	
	1	2	**Notes**
7	8	9	
14	15	16	
21	22	23	
28	29	30	
5	6	7	

October/November

28 Monday
1st ♏
Color: Lavender

Celtic Tree Month of Reed begins

29 Tuesday
1st ♏
☽ v/c 1:34 pm
☽ enters ♐ 5:58 pm
Color: Red

Ravens are messengers of the gods, so pay attention to them.

30 Wednesday
1st ♐
Color: White

31 Thursday
1st ♐
☽ v/c 10:30 am
☿ ℞ 11:41 am
☽ enters ♑ 10:38 pm
Color: Crimson

Samhain/Halloween
Mercury retrograde until November 20

1 Friday
1st ♑
♀ enters ♐ 4:25 pm
Color: White

All Saints' Day

Set in Eastern Daylight Time (EDT)

Samhain: Apples for the Beloved Dead

Samhain occurs near the apex of the zodiac sign Scorpio. Ruled by Mars in classical astrology and by Pluto in modern astrology, Scorpio is renowned for its energies of depth, mystery, and intensity. During this time of year, Witches willingly explore the mysteries of death and dying. While these forces are often surrounded by fear and superstition, we strive to understand both sides of nature's coin.

Gather your friends, family, or covenmates for the occasion. In addition to your standard ritual activities, give each participant a big apple and something to carve with. Ask everyone to inscribe the names of their beloved ancestors, human or animal, known or celebrity, recently departed or long-since passed. Venture outdoors at dusk to feel the ancestors of the land who still exist etherically. Encourage participants to silently meditate on these ancestors. When ready, ask everyone to speak a prayer to the departed that pays respect to those souls who have forged the way for us all. Offer the apples where deer and other critters can consume the fruit after the ancestors have taken their energies. *Memento mori.*

—Raven Digitalis

2 Saturday
1st ♑
Color: Brown

3 Sunday
1st ♑
☽ v/c 1:46 am
☽ enters ♒ 6:19 am
☿ enters ♎ 9:28 pm
Color: Yellow

Daylight Saving Time ends at 2 am

Eastern Standard Time (EST) begins November 3

November

○ Monday
1st ♒
2nd quarter 5:23 am
Color: Gray

Burn myrrh for consecration and a divine offering.

5 Tuesday
2nd ♒
☽ v/c 9:37 am
☽ enters ♓ 6:08 pm
Color: Maroon

Election Day (general)

6 Wednesday
2nd ♓
Color: Topaz

Samedi, or Baron Samedi, is a sophisticated loa of death and crossroads. Since everyone dies, he is a good friend to have.

7 Thursday
2nd ♓
☽ v/c 8:13 pm
Color: Turquoise

Samhain crossquarter day (Sun reaches 15° Scorpio)

8 Friday
2nd ♓
☿ enters ♐ 5:18 am
☽ enters ♈ 6:49 am
Color: Coral

---

138   Set in Eastern Standard Time (EST)

Mayan Hot Chocolate

Mayan spices and Ecuadorian peppers remove any hindrances as they heal our bodies, enabling chocolate to open our hearts to the euphoria of human connectivity.

1 cup cocoa nibs
2 T. chocolate liquor
½ cup coconut water
1 tsp. sweet chili (aji cachucha) powder
½ tsp. hot chili (aji ancho) powder
1 pinch black mole chili powder
8 cups milk
1 cup half-and-half
1 cup whipping cream
1 cinnamon stick, whole
2 balls of allspice, whole
1 vanilla bean, paste and shell divided
¼ cup honey or agave nectar

In a large saucepan, heat all but the chocolate on medium-high heat. Cook to a near boil. Whisk constantly to produce an even, frothy result. Add the chocolate and whisk vigorously for 1–3 minutes until the smooth emulsion forms froth. Pour into warmed cups and share with someone special.

—Estha K. V. McNevin

9 Saturday
2nd ♈
Color: Blue

10 Sunday
2nd ♈
☽ v/c 9:00 am
☽ enters ♉ 6:18 pm
Color: Gold

November

11 Monday
2nd ♉
Color: White

Veterans Day
Remembrance Day (Canada)

☺ Tuesday
2nd ♉
Full Moon 8:34 am
☽ v/c 10:48 am
Color: Scarlet

Mourning Moon

13 Wednesday
3rd ♉
☽ enters ♊ 3:46 am
Color: Yellow

Yellow accounts for joy, learning, concentration, air, flexibility, and travel.

14 Thursday
3rd ♊
Color: Green

15 Friday
3rd ♊
☽ v/c 6:40 am
☽ enters ♋ 11:15 am
♀ enters ♑ 11:36 pm
Color: Pink

The Ganges River in India is revered and used in funerary rites.

The Stolen Moon

A long time ago, three men stole the Moon from the sky and hung it in a tree like a lantern. All agreed that the Moon was theirs and that each man would take his share with him to his grave. Eventually, the men and the pieces of the Moon were reunited in the underworld. The bright light of the now-always-full Moon caused chaos among the spirits and demons who were used to living in darkness. Hearing the ruckus in the great below, St. Peter came down from heaven and put the Moon back in the sky, restoring order to the world.

The Moon belongs to all of us and gazes down without judgment or favoritism. Not a thing to be tamed or captured, she is a perfect example by which to live, always changing, adapting, and thus maintaining balance. At November's Full Moon, meditate on the many things we share as human beings, similarities to be celebrated as much as our diversity:

The Moon is yours, the Moon is mine.
In her changing face we find the Divine.

—Natalie Zaman

16 Saturday
3rd ♋
Color: Black

Willow goes with water and brings flexibility.

17 Sunday
3rd ♋
☽ v/c 3:14 pm
☽ enters ♌ 4:57 pm
Color: Orange

Set in Eastern Standard Time (EST)

November

18 Monday
3rd ♌
Color: Ivory

Hat-Mehit is the Egyptian goddess of fish. She wears one on her head and looks after aquatic life.

○ Tuesday
3rd ♌
♂ enters ♏ 2:40 am
☽ v/c 4:11 pm
4th quarter 4:11 pm
☽ enters ♍ 8:54 pm
Color: Red

20 Wednesday
4th ♍
☿ D 2:12 pm
Color: Brown

Aluminum corresponds to Mercury, air, and masculine energy. Use it for invisibility or relieving burdens.

21 Thursday
4th ♍
☽ v/c 10:31 pm
☽ enters ♎ 11:20 pm
Color: Purple

22 Friday
4th ♎
☉ enters ♐ 9:59 am
Color: Rose

Sun enters Sagittarius

Set in Eastern Standard Time (EST)

Ritual Garments of the Witch

A Witch's garment can mean different things to different Witches. Some prefer an embroidered, ornate flowing robe, some have gothic gowns or suits, and others feel just as Witchy in a T-shirt with magical symbols printed on it. Some Witches prefer to be dressed in nothing but the air around them. Ritual wear is how you present yourself to the other Witches you may be working with, and to the spirits and deities as well. If you can sew, there are lots of patterns and fabrics to choose in your local fabric store. I know some thrifty Witches who even shop the Halloween stores looking for robes on clearance. I've been known to work solitary rituals in my street clothes, but sometimes I drape a prayer shawl over my clothes. I also have several capes and robes that I reserve for public rituals, coven meetings, and gatherings that I have been to over the years. I like to wash my special ritual garments by hand with a gentle natural soap, and I usually add a sachet of lavender, sage, or other magical herbs to the wash. I like to allow them to dry in the sun and breeze if it's possible.

—Mickie Mueller

23 Saturday
4th ♎
☽ v/c 9:49 pm
Color: Indigo

Snakes symbolize life, death, and rebirth because they shed their skins.

24 Sunday
4th ♎
☽ enters ♏ 12:58 am
Color: Yellow

November/December

25 Monday
4th ♏
☽ v/c 12:30 pm
♀ enters ♑ 7:28 pm
Color: Silver

Celtic Tree Month of Elder begins

☿ Tuesday
4th ♏
☽ enters ♐ 3:11 am
New Moon 10:06 am
Color: Black

27 Wednesday
1st ♐
♆ D 7:32 am
Color: White

Juniper conveys protection.

28 Thursday
1st ♐
☽ v/c 5:50 am
☽ enters ♑ 7:33 am
Color: Crimson

Thanksgiving Day (US)

29 Friday
1st ♑
☽ v/c 10:57 pm
Color: Purple

30 Saturday
1st ♑
☽ enters ♒ 3:13 pm
Color: Blue

*The Great Serpent Mound in the
United States aligns with the summer solstice.*

1 Sunday
1st ♒
Color: Amber

Daisies are used in spells for love and divination.

December 2019

S	M	T	W
1	2	3	☾
8	9	10	11
15	16	17	☽
22	23	24	25
29	30	31	1
5	6	7	8

T	F	S	
5	6	7	**Notes**
☺	13	14	
19	20	21	
☾	27	28	
2	3	4	
9	10	11	

December

2 Monday
1st ≈
☽ v/c 7:27 am
♃ enters ♑ 1:20 pm
Color: Lavender

3 Tuesday
1st ≈
☽ enters ♓ 2:11 am
Color: Gray

*Tethur is a Celtic god of communication.
Pray to him for the right thing to say.*

☽ Wednesday
1st ♓
2nd quarter 1:58 am
Color: Yellow

*"Doing what you like is freedom. Liking
what you do is happiness."* —Frank Tyger

5 Thursday
2nd ♓
☽ v/c 3:15 am
☽ enters ♈ 2:44 pm
Color: White

6 Friday
2nd ♈
Color: Pink

Set in Eastern Standard Time (EST)

Oven-Roasted Peppers

This Yuletide favorite is beloved for brunch and is even better cold, according to some midday risers.

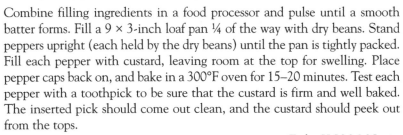

2 8-oz. packs of cream cheese, softened to room temperature
2 T. cornstarch
8 eggs
½ T. fresh dill
3 T. ranch dip mix
½ cup cheddar cheese, shredded
30–40 small sweet peppers: tops removed and saved, seeds rinsed out in sink, and peppers set out to dry
4–6 cups clay pastry pearls or dried pinto beans for blind baking

Combine filling ingredients in a food processor and pulse until a smooth batter forms. Fill a 9 × 3-inch loaf pan ¼ of the way with dry beans. Stand peppers upright (each held by the dry beans) until the pan is tightly packed. Fill each pepper with custard, leaving room at the top for swelling. Place pepper caps back on, and bake in a 300°F oven for 15–20 minutes. Test each pepper with a toothpick to be sure that the custard is firm and well baked. The inserted pick should come out clean, and the custard should peek out from the tops.

—Estha K. V. McNevin

7 Saturday
2nd ♈
☽ v/c 10:01 am
Color: Brown

8 Sunday
2nd ♈
☽ enters ♉ 2:29 am
Color: Gold

Birch wood represents birth and other beginnings, ideal for use in a nursery.

Set in Eastern Standard Time (EST)

December

9 Monday
2nd ♉
☿ enters ♐ 4:42 am
☽ v/c 8:13 pm
Color: Silver

Receptive stones include coral, emerald, jet, and pearl.

10 Tuesday
2nd ♉
☽ enters ♊ 11:47 am
Color: Red

11 Wednesday
2nd ♊
Color: Topaz

Cobalt produces a deep blue to ultraviolet color when mixed with glass. Cobalt glass enhances magical power.

☺ Thursday
2nd ♊
☽ v/c 12:12 am
Full Moon 12:12 am
☽ enters ♋ 6:23 pm
⚷ D 10:48 pm
Color: Purple

Long Nights Moon

13 Friday
3rd ♋
Color: Coral

Set in Eastern Standard Time (EST)

The Buried Moon

Once upon a time the Moon came down to earth. She was curious to gaze upon the bogs and marshes, for she had heard that they captured her reflection more beautifully than any other body of water. As she marveled at the bog, she spied a man. Frightened he might fall in and drown, she came closer, and bogles, wicked creatures of the marshlands, pulled her in. The Moon lay buried under water and weeds, and folk noticed that she was missing. They asked their wise woman what happened, and she told them to search the bogs. Spying a glimmer of light, they freed the Moon. Ever since, Luna shines most brightly over bogs and marshes, the better to protect those who pass through them in the dark. It's easy to appreciate the Moon when she is full, but even in her most shadowy phase, she is powerful. Every stage of her monthly metamorphosis has its own significance. Offer a blessing for her at the year's end, as you asked for a blessing at the year's beginning:

> Buried in dark, or crowned with light,
> I bless the Moon each and every night.

—Natalie Zaman

14 Saturday

3rd ♋
☽ v/c 10:57 am
☽ enters ♌ 10:56 pm
Color: Blue

Mount Kailash in Tibet has a path around it used for cleansing one's karma.

15 Sunday

3rd ♌
Color: Yellow

Set in Eastern Standard Time (EST)

December

16 Monday
3rd ♌
☽ v/c 5:10 pm
Color: White

Titanium is a light, strong metal. Used in space exploration,
it works well for astral projection and cosmic meditation.

17 Tuesday
3rd ♌
☽ enters ♍ 2:16 am
Color: Scarlet

Reshep is the Egyptian god of war.
He oversees battle and military actions.

○ Wednesday
3rd ♍
4th quarter 11:57 pm
Color: Brown

19 Thursday
4th ♍
☽ v/c 3:07 am
☽ enters ♎ 5:04 am
Color: Crimson

20 Friday
4th ♎
♀ enters ♒ 1:42 am
Color: Rose

The Stone Circle of Almendres in Portugal
has carvings of social and religious import.

Set in Eastern Standard Time (EST)

Yule: Rebirthing the Midwinter Child

The Holy Child is a spiritual archetype that takes numerous forms. Whether Jesus, Horus, Ganesha, or Sol Invictus, the Holy Child is most often aligned with the Sun's return. The winter solstice honors the rebirth of the holy sun (or holy son) and its associated archetypes. In many ways, this Child of Promise is aligned with the force of evolution, demonstrating the cyclical nature of reality and the world's continued advancement toward higher consciousness with each turn of the Wheel. On Midwinter night, invite the energy of the "crowned and conquering" Sun to bless the world with its bountiful, illuminating, and life-giving qualities. With a group of ritual participants, have everyone create their own list of qualities desired for humankind. These should consist of phrases whose energies can help create and sustain world peace, such as empathy, respect, humility, health, and joy. Use these written spells as part of the kindling for your Yule log, and dedicate the intentions to the Holy Child's return. While the papers and log burn, dance and sing Pagan chants and holiday tunes aligned with peace on earth.

—Raven Digitalis

21 Saturday

4th ♎
☽ v/c 6:45 am
☽ enters ♏ 7:57 am
☉ enters ♑ 11:19 pm
Color: Gray

Yule/Winter Solstice
Sun enters Capricorn

22 Sunday

4th ♏
☽ v/c 10:27 pm
Color: Orange

December

23 Monday
4th ♏
☽ enters ♐ 11:34 am
Color: Gray

Hanukkah begins (at sundown on December 22)
Between (Celtic Tree Month)

24 Tuesday
4th ♐
Color: Maroon

Christmas Eve
Celtic Tree Month of Birch begins

25 Wednesday
4th ♐
☽ v/c 6:18 am
☽ enters ♑ 4:45 pm
Color: Topaz

Christmas Day

☽ Thursday
4th ♑
New Moon 12:13 am
Color: Green

Kwanzaa begins
Boxing Day (Canada and UK)
Solar eclipse 12:13 am, 4° ♑ 07'

27 Friday
1st ♑
☽ v/c 4:03 pm
Color: Purple

Magenta draws in magnetism, mature femininity, and life purpose.

Deity Images Inspired by Spirit

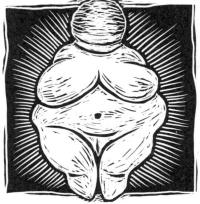

Most of the Witches I know have some kind of representation of deity on their altars or elsewhere in their homes. Most of these Witches don't actually worship the deity image itself but use it as a devotional piece to connect with the spirit of the deity. The images are only as powerful as what they represent for the Witch using them. Some use statues of specific gods and goddesses; others use a simple shell, stone, or other natural artifact, depending on personal preference. Framed art of a god or goddess can be placed on the altar or the wall behind it. I've been in many Witches' homes, and I've seen everything from museum reproductions and statues from garden centers to secondhand-store finds and even action figures! I've made my own primitively sculpted pieces from oven-bake clay for my deities, special pieces I used for years. There are many ways to display deity representations, often reflecting the magical tradition or gender identity of the Witch, who may use a single piece or multiple devotional pieces and in many varied combinations. There's no right or wrong way to honor deity in your magic as long as it's respectful to the deity.

—Mickie Mueller

28 Saturday
1st ♑
☽ enters ♒ 12:21 am
☿ enters ♑ 11:55 pm
Color: Indigo

29 Sunday
1st ♒
⚸ D 5:40 pm
Color: Gold

Set in Eastern Standard Time (EST)

December/January

30 Monday
1st ≈
☽ v/c 5:24 am
☽ enters ♓ 10:41 am
Color: Ivory

Hanukkah ends

31 Tuesday
1st ♓
Color: White

New Year's Eve

1 Wednesday
1st ♓
☽ v/c 9:14 pm
☽ enters ♈ 11:00 pm
Color: Yellow

New Year's Day
Kwanzaa ends

☽ Thursday
1st ♈
2nd quarter 11:45 pm
Color: Turquoise

Nickel corresponds to Mercury, earth, and feminine energy. It adds power to spells.

3 Friday
2nd ♈
♂ enters ♐ 4:37 am
☽ v/c 8:18 pm
Color: Pink

Set in Eastern Standard Time (EST)

4 Saturday
2nd ♈
☽ enters ♉ 11:15 am
Color: Gray

5 Sunday
2nd ♉
Color: Amber

"The great thing about getting older is that you don't lose all the other ages you've been." —Madeleine L'Engle

About the Contributors

ELIZABETH BARRETTE was the managing editor of *PanGaia* and has been involved with the Pagan community for twenty-five years. Her other writings include speculative fiction and gender studies. Her book *Composing Magic* explains how to write spells, rituals, and other liturgy. She lives in central Illinois and enjoys herbal landscaping and gardening for wildlife. Visit www.penultimateproductions.weebly.com and https://ysabetwordsmith.dreamwidth.org/.

BLAKE OCTAVIAN BLAIR is a shamanic practitioner, ordained minister, writer, Usui Reiki Master-Teacher, and musical artist. Blake blends various mystical traditions from both the East and West along with a reverence for the natural world into his own brand of spirituality. Blake lives in the New England region of the United States with his beloved husband. Visit him on the web at www.blakeoctavianblair.com or write him at blake@blakeoctavianblair.com.

KATHLEEN EDWARDS sold her first artworks in sixth grade—drawings of peace signs and flowers for ten cents each. She's been a book illustrator since 1991, and her work includes many Llewellyn publications. Her award-winning fine-art paintings have been widely exhibited and her graphic book, *Holy Stars!: Favorite Deities, Prophets, Saints & Sages from Around the World*, was published in 2009. See more of her work at www.kathleenedwardsartist.com.

MONICA CROSSON is the author of *The Magickal Family: Pagan Living in Harmony with Nature* (Llewellyn). She is a Master Gardener who lives in the beautiful Pacific Northwest with her husband, three kids, three goats, two dogs, two cats, many chickens, and Rosetta the donkey. She has been a practicing Witch for twenty-five years and is a member of Blue Moon Coven. Monica is a regular contributor to Llewellyn's annuals, calendars, and datebooks. She also enjoys writing fiction for young adults and is the author of *Summer Sage*.

AUTUMN DAMIANA is an author, artist, crafter, and amateur photographer. She is a Solitary Eclectic Cottage Witch who has been following her Pagan path for almost two decades and is a regular contributor to Llewellyn's annuals. Along with writing and making art, Autumn has a degree in early childhood education. She lives with her husband and doggy familiar in the beautiful San Francisco Bay Area. Visit her online at www.autumndamiana.com.

RAVEN DIGITALIS (Missoula, MT) is the author of *Esoteric Empathy, Shadow Magick Compendium, Planetary Spells & Rituals,* and *Goth Craft*. He is a Neopagan priest and cofounder of an Eastern Hellenistic nonprofit multicultural temple called Opus Aima Obscuræ. Trained in Eastern philosophies and Georgian Witchcraft, Raven has been an earth-based practitioner since 1999, a Priest since 2003, a Freemason since 2012, and an empath all his life. Visit www.ravendigitalis.com.

ESTHA K. V. MCNEVIN (Missoula, MT) is a priestess and Eastern Hellenistic oracle of Opus Aima Obscuræ. Since 2003, she has dedicated her time as a ceremonialist psychic, lecturer, freelance author, and artist. Amongst hosting public sabbats, Estha organizes annual philanthropic fundraisers, teaches classes, manages the temple farm, leads Full Moon spellcrafting ceremonies, and officiates for the women's divination rituals each Dark Moon. To learn more, please explore www.opusaimaobscurae.org and www.facebook.com/opusaimaobscurae.

MICKIE MUELLER loves to explore her spiritual path as a Witch in both her writing and illustrations. She's the author/illustrator of Voice of the Trees, illustrator of Mystical Cats Tarot and Magical Dogs Tarot, and author of *The Witch's Mirror* and *Llewellyn's Little Book of Halloween*. Mickie has been writing and illustrating for Llewellyn since 2007. Her internationally known art has appeared on television show sets on SyFy and Bravo.

DIANA RAJCHEL has practiced magic since childhood. She lives in San Francisco, where she runs the Emperor Norton Pagan Social and handles the oft-squirrely city spirit. She is the author of the Mabon and Samhain books in the Llewellyn Sabbat Essentials Series and of the Diagram Prize–nominee *Divorcing a Real Witch*.

CHARLYNN WALLS is the CEO/president of CEM, which oversees Witch School. A practitioner of the craft for over twenty years she currently resides in central Missouri with her family. She continues to share her knowledge by teaching at local festivals and continuing to produce articles for Llewellyn Publications.

NATALIE ZAMAN is the author of *Color and Conjure* and *Magical Destinations of the Northeast*. A regular contributor to various Llewellyn annual publications, she also writes the recurring feature Wandering Witch for *Witches & Pagans*. When not on the road, she's busy tending her magical back garden. Visit Natalie online at http://nataliezaman.blogspot.com.

Appendix

Daily Magical Influences
Each day is ruled by a planet with specific magical influences.
Monday (Moon): peace, healing, caring, psychic awareness
Tuesday (Mars): passion, courage, aggression, protection
Wednesday (Mercury): study, travel, divination, wisdom
Thursday (Jupiter): expansion, money, prosperity, generosity
Friday (Venus): love, friendship, reconciliation, beauty
Saturday (Saturn): longevity, endings, homes
Sunday (Sun): healing, spirituality, success, strength, protection

Color Correspondences
Colors are associated with each day, according to planetary influence.
Monday: gray, lavender, white, silver, ivory
Tuesday: red, white, black, gray, maroon, scarlet
Wednesday: yellow, brown, white, topaz
Thursday: green, turquoise, white, purple, crimson
Friday: white, pink, rose, purple, coral
Saturday: brown, gray, blue, indigo, black
Sunday: yellow, orange, gold, amber

Lunar Phases

Waxing, from New Moon to Full Moon, is the ideal time to do magic to draw things to you.

Waning, from Full Moon to New Moon, is a time for study, meditation, and magical work designed to banish harmful energies.

The Moon's Sign

The Moon continuously moves through each sign of the zodiac, from Aries to Pisces, staying about two and a half days in each sign. The Moon influences the sign it inhabits, creating different energies that affect our day-to-day lives.

Aries: Good for starting things. Things occur rapidly but quickly pass. People tend to be argumentative and assertive.

Taurus: Things begun now last longest, tend to increase in value, and become hard to change. Brings out an appreciation for beauty and sensory experience.

Gemini: Things begun now are easily changed by outside influence. Time for shortcuts, communication, games, and fun.

Cancer: Stimulates emotional rapport between people. Supports growth and nurturing. Tend to domestic concerns.

Leo: Draws emphasis to the self, to central ideas or institutions, away from connections with others and emotional needs.

Virgo: Favors accomplishment of details and commands from higher up. Focus on health, hygiene, and daily schedules.

Libra: Favors cooperation, compromise, social activities, balance, friendship, and partnership.

Scorpio: Increases awareness of psychic power. Precipitates psychic crises and ends connections thoroughly. People have a tendency to brood and become secretive.

Sagittarius: Encourages confidence and flights of imagination. This is an adventurous, philosophical, and athletic Moon sign. Favors expansion and growth.

Capricorn: Develops strong structure. Focus on traditions, responsibilities, and obligations. A good time to set boundaries and rules.

Aquarius: Rebellious energy. Time to break habits and make abrupt change. Personal freedom and individuality is the focus.

Pisces: The focus is on dreaming, nostalgia, intuition, and psychic impressions. A good time for spiritual or philanthropic activities.

Gemstones

Gemstones can be utilized for a variety of purposes and intentions.
Amber: ambition, balance, clarity, healing, protection, success
Amethyst: awareness, harmony, love, spirituality, protection
Citrine: beginnings, change, clarity, goals, goodness, rebirth, sleep
Emerald: clairvoyance, enchantment, jealousy, luck, spirits, wishes
Hematite: balance, grounding, knowledge, negativity, power, strength
Jade: abundance, dream work, money, nurture, peace, well-being, wisdom
Lodestone: attraction, fidelity, grounding, relationships, willpower
Moonstone: destiny, divination, intuition, knowledge, light, sleep
Obsidian: afterlife, aggression, death, fear, grounding, growth, obstacles
Quartz: awareness, clarity, communication, guidance, healing, rebirth
Ruby: compassion, connections, happiness, love, loyalty, passion, respect
Sapphire: astral realm, dedication, emotions, faith, improvement, insight
Tiger's Eye: battle, clarity, desire, energy, purification, strength, youth
Topaz: adaptability, courage, instrospection, loss, prosperity, wisdom
Tourmaline: attraction, business, consciousness, guidance, psychic ability
Turquoise: calm, change, creativity, dream work, empathy, energy, goals, healing, unity

Chakras

Chakras are spiritual energy centers located along the middle of the body.
Root Chakra: Activate with red. Balance with black.
Associated with comfort, grounding, security, support.
Sacral Chakra: Activate with orange. Balance with brown.
Associated with creativity, desire, freedom, passion.
Solar Plexus Chakra: Activate with yellow. Balance with brown.
Associated with confidence, power, transformation, willpower.
Heart Chakra: Activate with green. Balance with pink, rose.
Associated with beauty, compassion, healing, love, mindfulness.
Throat Chakra: Activate with blue. Balance with turquoise.
Associated with communication, inspiration, release, truth.
Forehead Chakra: Activate with indigo. Balance with white.
Associated with clarity, illumination, intuition, visions, wisdom.
Crown Chakra: Activate with violet, purple. Balance with gold, white.
Associated with consciousness, cosmic energy, enlightenment, knowledge, spirituality.

Herbs

Herbs are useful in spells, rituals, cooking and Kitchen Witchery, health, beauty, and crafts and have many common magical correspondences.

Basil: defense, home, love, prosperity, protection, purification, success
Borage: authority, business, happinesss, money, power, purification
Carnation: confidence, creativity, healing, protection, strength, truth
Chamomile: balance, beauty, calm, dream work, gentleness, peace, sleep
Clover: community, friendship, kindness, luck, wealth, youth
Daffodil: afterlife, beauty, faeries, fertility, luck, spirits
Daisy: beauty, cheerfulness, divination, innocence, love, pleasure
Dandelion: awareness, clarity, emotions, freedom, the mind, wishes
Fennel: aggression, courage, energy, stimulation, protection, strength
Fern: banishing, concentration, money, power, protection, release, spirits
Gardenia: comfort, compassion, the home, marriage, peace, true love
Garlic: anxiety, banishing, defense, healing, improvement, weather
Geranium: balance, concentration, fertility, forgiveness, healing
Honeysuckle: affection, gentleness, happiness, optimism, psychic ability
Ivy: animals, attachments, fertility, fidelity, growth, honor, secrets, security
Jasmine: binding, desire, dream work, grace, prosperity, relationships
Lavender: calm, creativity, friendship, peace, purification, sensitivity, sleep
Lilac: adaptability, beauty, clairvoyance, divination, emotions, spirits
Marigold: authority, awareness, endurance, healing, longevity, visions
Marjoram: comfort, family, innocence, loneliness, love, purification
Peppermint: action, awaken, clarity, intelligence, the mind, stimulation
Poppy: astral realm, dream work, fertility, luck, prosperity, sleep, visions
Rose: affection, attraction, blessings, fidelity, love, patience, sexuality
Rosemary: banishing, binding, defense, determination, healing, memory, protection
Sage: consecration, grounding, guidance, memory, obstacles, reversal
Thyme: confidence, growth, happiness, honesty, purification, sorrow
Violet: beauty, changes, endings, heartbreak, hope, lust, passion, shyness
Yarrow: awareness, banishing, calm, challenges, power, protection, success

See *Llewellyn's Complete Book of Correspondences* by Sandra Kynes for a comprehensive catalog of correspondences.

2019 Eclipses

January 5, 8:28 pm; Solar eclipse 15° ♑ 25'
January 21, 12:16 am; Lunar eclipse 0° ♌ 52'
July 2, 3:16 pm; Solar eclipse 10° ♋ 38'
July 16, 5:38 pm; Lunar eclipse 24° ♑ 04'
December 26, 12:13 am; Solar eclipse 4° ♑ 07'

2019 Full Moons

Cold Moon: January 21, 12:16 am
Quickening Moon: February 19, 10:54 am
Storm Moon: March 20, 9:43 pm
Wind Moon: April 19, 7:12 am
Flower Moon: May 18, 5:11 pm
Strong Sun Moon: June 17, 4:31 am
Blessing Moon: July 16, 5:38 pm
Corn Moon: August 15, 8:29 am
Harvest Moon: September 14, 12:33 am
Blood Moon: October 13, 5:08 pm
Mourning Moon: November 12, 8:34 am
Long Nights Moon: December 12, 12:12 am

Planetary Retrogrades in 2019

Planet		Retrograde			Direct	
Uranus	℞	08/07/18	12:48 pm	— Direct	01/06/19	3:27 pm
Mercury	℞	03/05/19	1:19 pm	— Direct	03/28/19	9:59 am
Jupiter	℞	04/10/19	1:01 pm	— Direct	08/11/19	9:37 am
Pluto	℞	04/24/19	2:48 pm	— Direct	10/03/19	2:39 am
Saturn	℞	04/29/19	8:54 pm	— Direct	09/18/19	4:47 am
Neptune	℞	06/21/19	10:36 am	— Direct	11/27/19	7:32 pm
Mercury	℞	07/07/19	7:14 pm	— Direct	07/31/19	11:58 pm
Uranus	℞	08/11/19	10:27 pm	— Direct	01/10/20	8:49 pm
Mercury	℞	10/31/19	11:41 am	— Direct	11/20/19	2:12 pm

Set in Eastern Time. All times corrected for Daylight Saving Time.

Moon Void-of-Course Data for 2019

JANUARY

Last Aspect Date	Time	New Sign	New Time
1	5:26 pm	♐	3:58 am
4	12:41 pm	♑	1:55 pm
7	1:20 am	♒	1:46 pm
9	11:53 am	♓	2:44 pm
11	9:25 am	♈	3:18 pm
14	10:56 am	♉	1:31 pm
16	1:34 pm	♊	8:00 pm
18	8:32 pm	♋	10:44 pm
20	8:50 pm	♌	10:54 pm
22	8:19 pm	♍	10:22 pm
24	8:50 am	♎	11:02 pm
27	12:21 am	♏	2:31 am
28	5:39 pm	♐	9:33 am
31	5:33 pm	♑	7:47 pm

FEBRUARY

Last Aspect Date	Time	New Sign	New Time
3	5:53 am	♒	8:03 am
5	6:59 pm	♓	9:02 pm
7	5:14 pm	♈	9:34 am
10	6:48 pm	♉	8:28 pm
12	5:26 pm	♊	4:32 am
15	7:48 am	♋	9:03 am
17	9:17 am	♌	10:21 am
19	8:51 am	♍	9:47 am
20	8:52 pm	♎	9:17 am
23	10:11 am	♏	10:56 am
25	7:14 am	♐	4:19 pm
28	1:17 am	♑	1:48 am

MARCH

Last Aspect Date	Time	New Sign	New Time
2	1:47 pm	♒	2:06 pm
5	3:05 am	♓	3:11 am
7	2:08 pm	♈	3:27 pm
9	12:14 pm	♉	3:10 am
12	5:31 am	♊	11:48 am
14	8:30 am	♋	5:49 pm
16	2:03 pm	♌	8:57 pm
18	11:19 am	♍	9:41 pm
20	11:22 am	♎	9:28 pm
22	2:10 pm	♏	10:16 pm
24	10:24 pm	♐	2:06 am
26	10:37 am	♑	10:07 am
29	8:05 pm	♒	9:46 pm
31	11:02 pm	4/1 ♓	10:48 am

APRIL

Last Aspect Date	Time	New Sign	New Time
3/31	11:02 pm	1 ♓	10:48 am
3	11:36 am	♈	10:56 pm
5	10:15 pm	♉	9:06 am
8	4:29 am	♊	5:15 pm
10	1:27 pm	♋	11:31 pm
12	7:33 pm	♌	3:50 am
14	9:38 pm	♍	6:14 am
17	12:29 am	♎	7:22 am
19	7:12 am	♏	8:41 am
21	12:00 am	♐	11:59 am
23	7:44 am	♑	6:50 pm
25	3:48 pm	♒	5:27 am
28	5:44 am	♓	6:11 am
30	5:57 pm	5/1 ♈	6:24 am

MAY

Last Aspect Date	Time	New Sign	New Time
4/30	5:57 pm	1 ♈	6:24 am
3	4:47 am	♉	4:18 pm
5	11:10 am	♊	11:40 pm
7	7:50 pm	♋	5:06 am
9	10:06 pm	♌	9:14 am
12	8:24 am	♍	12:22 pm
14	1:19 pm	♎	2:51 pm
16	5:31 am	♏	5:26 pm
18	5:11 pm	♐	9:21 pm
20	1:05 pm	♑	3:56 am
22	11:58 pm	♒	1:49 pm
25	8:51 am	♓	2:08 am
28	12:21 am	♈	2:32 pm
30	11:08 am	31 ♉	12:43 am

JUNE

Last Aspect Date	Time	New Sign	New Time
1	6:53 pm	2 ♊	7:48 am
4	11:42 am	♋	12:17 pm
6	10:10 am	♌	3:16 pm
8	5:23 pm	♍	5:45 pm
10	8:01 am	♎	8:29 pm
12	11:15 am	♏	12:02 am
14	3:46 pm	♐	5:03 am
17	4:31 am	♑	12:13 pm
19	7:19 am	♒	10:01 pm
21	10:02 am	♓	10:01 am
24	7:10 pm	♈	10:38 pm
27	3:51 am	♉	9:32 am
29	2:38 pm	♊	5:09 pm

JULY

Last Aspect Date	Time	New Sign	New Time
1	5:48 pm	♋	9:24 pm
3	10:25 am	♌	11:19 pm
5	2:24 am	♍	12:25 pm
7	12:50 pm	♎	2:07 am
9	3:36 pm	♏	5:29 am
11	8:28 pm	♐	11:05 am
13	9:30 pm	♑	7:05 pm
16	5:38 pm	♒	5:19 am
18	11:53 am	♓	5:19 pm
22	4:34 am	♈	6:02 am
24	10:48 am	♉	5:42 pm
27	12:28 am	♊	2:29 am
28	11:24 am	♋	7:31 am
30	11:32 pm	31 ♌	9:18 am

AUGUST

Last Aspect Date	Time	New Sign	New Time
1	4:48 pm	2 ♍	9:20 am
4	12:27 am	♎	9:30 am
6	3:36 am	♏	11:31 am
8	10:58 am	♐	4:35 pm
10	3:50 pm	♑	12:50 am
12	6:11 pm	♒	11:35 am
15	9:02 pm	♓	11:49 pm
17	6:35 pm	18 ♈	12:33 pm
21	12:06 am	♉	12:37 am
22	5:33 pm	23 ♊	10:34 am
25	12:58 am	♋	5:05 pm
27	4:55 am	♌	7:53 pm
28	8:07 pm	29 ♍	7:57 pm
31	4:46 am	31 ♎	7:08 pm

SEPTEMBER

Last Aspect Date	Time	New Sign	New Time
2	4:34 am	2 ♏	7:35 pm
4	6:58 am	4 ♐	11:08 pm
6	12:03 pm	7 ♑	6:37 am
9	4:30 am	9 ♒	5:24 pm
11	1:22 am	12 ♓	5:52 am
14	12:33 am	14 ♈	6:32 pm
16	12:03 pm	17 ♉	6:31 am
19	9:57 am	19 ♊	4:58 pm
21	10:41 pm	22 ♋	12:50 am
23	6:05 pm	24 ♌	5:19 am
25	12:14 pm	26 ♍	6:37 am
27	11:58 pm	28 ♎	6:03 am
29	10:06 pm	30 ♏	5:42 am

OCTOBER

Last Aspect Date	Time	New Sign	New Time
2	5:46 am	2 ♐	7:44 am
4	3:34 am	4 ♑	1:43 pm
6	7:25 pm	6 ♒	11:42 pm
8	2:27 pm	9 ♓	12:05 pm
11	5:55 am	12 ♈	12:46 am
13	5:59 pm	14 ♉	12:24 pm
16	4:37 am	16 ♊	10:30 pm
18	10:14 pm	19 ♋	6:43 am
21	8:39 am	21 ♌	12:29 pm
23	5:14 am	23 ♍	3:29 pm
25	9:00 am	25 ♎	4:20 pm
27	4:22 am	27 ♏	4:29 pm
29	1:34 pm	29 ♐	5:58 pm
31	10:30 am	31 ♑	10:38 pm

NOVEMBER

Last Aspect Date	Time	New Sign	New Time
3	1:46 am	3 ♒	6:19 am
5	9:37 am	5 ♓	6:08 pm
7	8:13 pm	8 ♈	6:49 am
10	9:00 am	10 ♉	6:18 pm
12	10:48 am	13 ♊	3:46 am
15	6:40 am	15 ♋	11:15 am
17	3:14 pm	17 ♌	4:57 pm
19	4:11 pm	19 ♍	8:54 pm
21	10:31 pm	21 ♎	11:20 pm
23	9:49 pm	24 ♏	12:58 am
25	12:30 pm	26 ♐	3:11 am
28	5:50 am	28 ♑	7:33 am
29	10:57 pm	30 ♒	3:13 pm

DECEMBER

Last Aspect Date	Time	New Sign	New Time
2	7:27 am	3 ♓	2:11 am
5	3:15 am	5 ♈	2:44 pm
7	10:01 am	8 ♉	2:29 am
9	8:13 pm	10 ♊	11:47 am
12	12:12 am	12 ♋	6:23 pm
14	10:57 pm	14 ♌	10:56 pm
16	5:10 pm	17 ♍	2:16 am
19	3:07 am	19 ♎	5:04 am
21	6:45 pm	21 ♏	7:57 am
22	10:27 pm	23 ♐	11:34 am
25	6:18 am	25 ♑	4:45 pm
27	4:03 pm	28 ♒	12:21 am
30	5:24 pm	30 ♓	10:41 am

Set in Eastern Time. All times corrected for Daylight Saving Time.

Notes

Notes

Notes